EVIL AND WORLD ORDER

WORLD PERSPECTIVES

Volumes already published

WORLD PERSPECTIVES · *Volume Forty-nine*

Planned and Edited by **RUTH NANDA ANSHEN**

EVIL AND
WORLD ORDER

WILLIAM IRWIN THOMPSON

1817

HARPER & ROW, PUBLISHERS

New York, Hagerstown, San Francisco, London

Permission granted by the following publishers for use of material under copyright is gratefully acknowledged: For "Meditation on the Dark Ages, Past and Present," *The New Alchemy Journal*, Vol. III, 1975. For "We Become What We Hate," *The New York Times*, copyright © 1971 by The New York Times Company. For "Three Wise Men of Gotham," which first appeared as "Technological Liberalism" and "Technology: the Final Solution" in *The Canadian Forum*. For "Occulture: Out of Sight, Out of Mind," which first appeared as "Alternate Realities" in *The New York Times Book Review*, copyright © by The New York Times Company, 1972. For material in "Introductions to Findhorn": Part I, which first appeared as the Foreword to *The Findhorn Garden* by The Findhorn Community, Harper & Row, Publishers, copyright © 1975 by The Findhorn Foundation; and Part II, which first appeared as "Mysticism and Science" in *The New Age Journal*. For "Freedom, Evil, and Comedy," which first appeared in *The Tulane Drama Review*, Spring, 1965, Vol. 9, No. 3. For "The Ends of Art," which first appeared as "Art in the Doorway Between Two Worlds" in *The Los Angeles Times Book Review*. For lines from Richmond Lattimore's translation of Homer's *Iliad*, University of Chicago Press. For lines from Phillip Wayne's translation of Goethe's *Faust*, reprinted by permission of Penguin Books. For lines from T. S. Eliot's *The Waste Land*, from *The Collected Poems 1909–1962*, reprinted by permission of Harcourt Brace Jovanovich, Inc. For material from José Delgado's *The Physical Control of the Mind: Toward a Psychocivilized Society*, reprinted by permission of Harper & Row, Publishers.

FIRST EDITION

Library of Congress Cataloging in Publication Data

Thompson, William Irwin.
  Evil and world order.

  (World perspectives ; v. 49)
  Includes index.
  CONTENTS: Meditation on the Dark Ages, past and present.—We become what we hate.—Three wise men of Gotham. [etc.]
    1. Civilization, Modern—1950–   —Addresses, essays, lectures. 2. Technology and civilization—Addresses, essays, lectures. I. Title.
  CB428.T46 1976   909.82   74-20417
  ISBN 0-06-014276-6

76 77 78 79 10 9 8 7 6 5 4 3 2 1

Contents

World Perspectives

What This Series Means

It is the thesis of *World Perspectives* that man is in the process of developing a new consciousness which, in spite of his apparent spiritual and moral captivity, can eventually lift the human race above and beyond the fear, ignorance, and isolation which beset it today. It is to this nascent consciousness, to this concept of man born out of a universe perceived through a fresh vision of reality, that *World Perspectives* is dedicated.

My Introduction to this Series is not of course to be construed as a prefatory essay for each individual book. These few pages simply attempt to set forth the general aim and purpose of the Series as a whole. They try to point to the principle of permanence within change and to define the essential nature of man, as presented by those scholars who have been invited to participate in this intellectual and spiritual movement.

Man has entered a new era of evolutionary history, one in which rapid change is a dominant consequence. He is contending with a fundamental change, since he has intervened in the evolutionary process. He must now better appreciate this fact and then develop the wisdom to direct the process toward his fulfillment rather than toward his destruction. As he learns to apply his understanding of the physical world for practical purposes, he is, in reality, extending his innate capacity and augmenting his ability and his need to communicate as well as his ability to think and to create. And as a result, he is substituting a goal-directed evolutionary process in his struggle against environmental hardship for the slow, but effective, biological evolution which produced modern man through mutation and natural selection. By intelligent intervention in the evolutionary process man has greatly accelerated and greatly expanded the range of his possibilities. But he has not changed the basic fact that it remains a trial and error process, with the danger of taking paths that lead to sterility of mind and heart, moral apathy and intellectual inertia; and even producing social dinosaurs unfit to live in an evolving world. WHO IS HE TO MAKE THIS JUDGEMENT?

Only those spiritual and intellectual leaders of our epoch who have a paternity in this extension of man's horizons are invited to participate in the Series: those who are aware of the truth that beyond the divisiveness among men there exists a primordial unitive power since we are all bound together by a common humanity more fundamental than any unity of dogma; those who recognize that the centrifugal force which has scattered and atomized mankind must be replaced by an integrating structure and process capable of bestowing meaning and purpose on existence; those who realize that science itself, when not inhibited by the limitations of its own methodology, when chastened and humbled, commits man to an indeterminate range of yet undreamed consequences that may flow from it.

Virtually all of our disciplines have relied on conceptions which are now incompatible with the Cartesian axiom, and with the static world view we once derived from it. For underlying the new ideas, including those of modern physics, is a unifying order, but it is not causality; it is purpose, and not the purpose of the universe and of man, but the purpose *in* the universe and *in* man. In other words, we seem to inhabit a world of dynamic process and structure. Therefore we need

WE EXPERTS WILL DEFINE FOR YOU LITTLE PEOPLE
A NEW PURPOSE AND STRUCTURE

a calculus of potentiality rather than one of probability, a dialectic of polarity, one in which unity and diversity are redefined as simultaneous and necessary poles of the same essence. — *SOUNDS MORE LIKE INSANITY TO ME.*

Our situation is new. No civilization has previously had to face the challenge of scientific specialization, and our response must be new. Thus this Series is committed to ensure that the spiritual and moral needs of a man as a human being and the scientific and intellectual resources at his command for *life* may be brought into a productive, meaningful and creative harmony. — *WHO DEFINES THESE NEEDS — YOUR PSYCHIATRIST?*

In a certain sense we may say that man now has regained his former geocentric position in the universe. For a picture of the Earth has been made available from distant space, from the lunar desert, and the sheer isolation of the Earth has become plain. This is as new and as powerful an idea in history as any that has ever been born in man's consciousness. We are all becoming seriously concerned with our natural environment. And this concern is not only the result of the warnings given by biologists, ecologists and conservationists. Rather it is the result of a deepening awareness that something new has happened, that the planet Earth is a unique and precious place. Indeed, it may not be a mere coincidence that this awareness should have been born at the exact moment when man took his first step into outer space.

This Series endeavors to point to a reality of which scientific theory has revealed only one aspect. It is the commitment to this reality that lends universal intent to a scientist's most original and solitary thought. By acknowledging this frankly we shall restore science to the great family of human aspirations by which men hope to fulfill themselves in the world community as thinking and sentient beings. For our problem is to discover a principle of differentiation and yet relationship lucid enough to justify and to purify scientific, philosophic and all other knowledge, both discursive and intuitive, by accepting their interdependence. This is the crisis in consciousness made articulate through the crisis in science. This is the new awakening.

Each volume presents the thought and belief of its author and points to the way in which religion, philosophy, art, science, economics, politics and history may constitute that form of human activity which takes the fullest and most precise account of variousness, possibility, complexity and difficulty. Thus *World Perspectives* endeavors to define that ecumenical power of the mind and heart which enables man through his mysterious greatness to re-create his life.

This Series is committed to a re-examination of all those sides of human endeavor which the specialist was taught to believe he could safely leave aside. It attempts to show the structural kinship between subject and object; the indwelling of the one in the other. It interprets present and past events impinging on human life in our growing World Age and world consciousness and envisages what man may yet attain when summoned by an unbending inner necessity to the quest of what is most exalted in him. Its purpose is to offer new vistas in terms of world and human development while refusing to betray the intimate correlation between universality and individuality, dynamics and form, freedom and destiny. Each author deals with the increasing realization that spirit and nature are not separate and apart; that intuition and reason must regain their convergence as the means of perceiving and fusing inner being with outer reality.

World Perspectives endeavors to show that the conception of wholeness, unity, organism is a higher and more concrete conception than that of matter and energy. Thus an enlarged meaning of life, of biology, not as it is revealed in the test tube of the laboratory but as it is experienced within the organism of life itself, is attempted in this Series. For the principle of life consists in the tension which connects spirit with the realm of matter, symbiotically joined. The element of life is dominant in the very texture of nature, thus rendering life, biology, a transempirical science. The laws of life have their origin beyond their mere physical manifestations and compel us to consider their spiritual source. In fact, the widening of the conceptual framework has not only served to restore order within the respective branches of knowledge, but has also disclosed analogies in man's position regarding the analysis and synthesis of experience in apparently separated domains of knowledge, suggesting the possibility of an ever more embracing objective description of the meaning of life.

Knowledge, it is shown in these books, no longer consists in a manipulation of man and nature as opposite forces, nor in the reduction of data to mere statistical order, but is a means of liberating mankind from the destructive power of fear, pointing the way toward the goal of the rehabilitation of the human will and the rebirth of faith and confidence in the human person. The works published also endeavor to reveal that the cry for patterns, systems and authorities is growing less insistent as the desire grows stronger in both East and West for the recovery of a dignity, integrity and self-realization which are the inalienable rights of man who may now guide change by means of conscious purpose in the light of rational experience.

The volumes in this Series endeavor to demonstrate that only in a society in which awareness of the problems of science exists, can its discoveries start great waves of change in human culture, and in such a manner that these discoveries may deepen and not erode the sense of universal human community. The differences in the disciplines, their epistemological exclusiveness, the variety of historical experiences, the differences of traditions, of cultures, of languages, of the arts, should be protected and preserved. But the interrelationship and unity of the whole should at the same time be accepted.

The authors of *World Perspectives* are of course aware that the ultimate answers to the hopes and fears which pervade modern society rest on the moral fibre of man, and on the wisdom and responsibility of those who promote the course of its development. But moral decisions cannot dispense with an insight into the interplay of the objective elements which offer and limit the choices made. Therefore an understanding of what the issues are, though not a sufficient condition, is a necessary prerequisite for directing action toward constructive solutions.

Other vital questions explored relate to problems of international understanding as well as to problems dealing with prejudice and the resultant tensions and antagonisms. The growing perception and responsibility of our World Age point to the new reality that the individual person and the collective person supplement and integrate each other; that the thrall of totalitarianism of both left and right has been shaken in the universal desire to recapture the authority of truth and human totality. Mankind can finally place its trust not in a proletarian authoritarianism, not in a secularized humanism, both of which have betrayed the spiritual property right of history, but in a sacramental brotherhood and in the unity of knowledge. This new consciousness has created a widening of human horizons beyond every parochialism, and a revolution in human thought comparable to the basic assumption, among the ancient Greeks, of the sovereignty of reason; corresponding to the great effulgence of the moral conscience articulated by the Hebrew prophets; analogous to the fundamental assertions of Christianity; or to the beginning of the new scientific era, the era of the science of dynamics, the experimental foundations of which were laid by Galileo in the Renaissance.

An important effort of this Series is to re-examine the contradictory meanings and applications which are given today to such terms as democracy, freedom, justice, love, peace, brotherhood and God. The purpose of such inquiries is to clear the way for the foundation of a genuine *world* history not in terms of nation or race or culture but in terms of man in relation to God, to himself, his fellow man and the universe, that reach beyond immediate self-interest. For the meaning of the World Age consists in respecting man's hopes and dreams which lead to a deeper understanding of the basic values of all peoples.

World Perspectives is planned to gain insight into the meaning of man, who not only is determined by history but who also determines history. History is to be understood as concerned not only with the life of man on this planet but as including also such cosmic influences as interpenetrate our human world. This generation is discovering that history does not conform to the social optimism of modern civilization and that the organization of human communities and the establishment of freedom and peace are not only intellectual achievements but spiritual and moral achievements as well, demanding a cherishing of the wholeness of human personality, the "unmediated wholeness of feeling and thought," and constituting a never-ending challenge to man, emerging from the abyss of meaninglessness and suffering, to be renewed and replenished in the totality of his life.

Justice itself, which has been "in a state of pilgrimage and crucifixion" and now is being slowly liberated from the grip of social and political demonologies in the East as well as in the West, begins to question its own premises. The modern revolutionary movements which have challenged the sacred institutions of society by protecting injustice in the name of social justice are here examined and reevaluated.

In the light of this, we have no choice but to admit that the *un*freedom against which freedom is measured must be retained with it, namely, that the aspect of truth out of which the night view appears to emerge, the darkness of our time, is as little abandonable as is man's subjective advance. Thus the two sources of man's consciousness are inseparable, not as dead but as living and complementary, an aspect of that "principle of complementarity" through which Niels Bohr has sought to unite the quantum and the wave, both of which constitute the very fabric of life's radiant energy.

There is in mankind today a counterforce to the sterility and danger of a quantitative, anonymous mass culture; a new, if sometimes imperceptible, spiritual sense of convergence toward human and world unity on the basis of the sacredness of each human person and respect for the plurality of cultures. There is a growing awareness that equality may not be evaluated in mere numerical terms but is proportionate and analogical in its reality. For when equality is equated with interchangeability, individuality is negated and the human person transmuted into a faceless mask.

We stand at the brink of an age of a world in which human life presses forward to actualize new forms. The false separation of man and nature, of time and space, of freedom and security, is acknowledged, and we are faced with a new vision of man in his organic unity and of history offering a richness and diversity of equality and majesty of scope hitherto unprecedented. In relating the accumulated wisdom of man's spirit to the new reality of the World Age, in articulating its thought and belief, *World Perspectives* seeks to encourage a renaissance of hope in society and of pride in man's decision as to what his destiny will be.

Man has certainly contrived to change the environment, but subject to the new processes involved in this change, the same process of selection continues to operate. The environment has changed partly in a physical and geographical sense, but more particularly from the knowledge we now possess. The Biblical story of Adam and Eve contains a deep lesson, which a casual reading hardly reveals. Once the "fruit of the Tree of Knowledge" has been eaten, the world is changed. The new world is dictated by the knowledge itself, not of course by an edict of God. The Biblical story has further interest in that the new world is said to be much worse than the former idyllic state of ignorance. Today we are beginning to wonder whether this might not also be true. Yet we are uneasy, apprehensive, and our fears lead to the collapse of civilizations. Thus we turn to the truth that knowledge and life are indivisible, even as life and death are inseparable. We *are* what we know and think and feel; we are linked with history, with the world, with the universe, and faith in *Life* creates its own verification.

World Perspectives is committed to the recognition that all great changes are preceded by a vigorous intellectual re-evaluation and reorganization. Our authors are aware that the sin of *hubris* may be avoided by showing that the creative process itself is not a free activity if by free we mean arbitrary, or unrelated to cosmic law. For the creative process in the human mind, the developmental process in organic nature and the basic laws of the inorganic realm may be but varied expressions of a universal formative process. Thus *World Perspectives* hopes to show that although the present apocalyptic period is one of exceptional tensions, there is also at work an exceptional movement toward a compensating unity which refuses to violate the ultimate moral power at work in the universe, that very power upon which all human effort must at last depend. In this way we may come to understand that there exists an inherent interdependence of spiritual and mental growth which, though conditioned by circumstances, is never determined by circumstances. In this way the great plethora of human knowledge may be correlated with an insight into the nature of human nature by being attuned to the wide and deep range of human thought and human experience.

Incoherence is the result of the present disintegrative processes in education. Thus the need for *World Perspectives* expresses itself in the recognition that natural and man-made ecological systems require as much study as isolated particles and elementary reactions. For there is a basic correlation of elements in nature as in man which cannot be separated, which compose each other and alter each other mutually. Thus we hope to widen appropriately our conceptual framework of reference. For our epistemological problem consists in our finding the proper balance between our lack of an all-embracing principle relevant to our way of evaluating life and in our power to express ourselves in a logically consistent manner.

Our Judeo-Christian and Greco-Roman heritage, our Hellenic tradition, has compelled us to think in exclusive categories. But our *experience* challenges us to recognize a totality richer and far more complex than the average observer could have suspected—a totality which compels him to think in ways which the logic of dichotomies denies. We are summoned to revise fundamentally our ordinary ways of conceiving experience, and thus, by expanding our vision and by accepting those forms of thought which also include nonexclusive categories, the mind is then able to grasp what it was incapable of grasping or accepting before.

Nature operates out of necessity; there is no alternative in nature, no will, no freedom, no choice as there is for man. Man must have convictions and values to live for, and this also is recognized and accepted by those scientists who are at the same time philosophers. For they then realize that duty and devotion to our task, be it a task of acting or of understanding, will become weaker and rarer unless guidance is sought in a metaphysics that transcends our historical and scientific views or in a religion that transcends and yet pervades the work we are carrying on in the light of day.

For the nature of knowledge, whether scientific or ontological, consists in reconciling *meaning* and *being*. And *being* signifies nothing other than the actualization of potentiality, self-realization which keeps in tune with the transformation. This leads to experience in terms of the individual; and to organization and patterning in terms of the universe. Thus organism and world actualize themselves simultaneously.

And so we may conclude that organism is *being* enduring in time, in fact in eternal time, since it does not have its beginning with procreation, nor with birth, nor does it end with death. Energy and matter in whatever form they may manifest themselves are transtemporal and transspatial and are therefore metaphysical. Man as man is summoned to know what is right and what is wrong, for emptied of such knowledge he is unable to decide what is better or what is worse.

World Perspectives hopes to show that human society is different from animal societies, which, having reached a certain stage, are no longer progressive but are dominated by routine and repetition. Thus man has discovered his own nature, and with this self-knowledge he has left the state of nonage and entered manhood. For he is the only creature who is able to say not only "no" to life but "yes" and to make for himself a life that is human. In this decision lie his burden and his greatness. For the power of life or death lies not only in the tongue but in man's recently acquired ability to destroy or to create life itself, and therefore he is faced with unlimited and unprecedented choices for good and for evil that dominate our time. Our common concern is the very destiny of the human race. For man has now intervened in the process of evolution, a power not given to the pre-Socratics, nor to Aristotle, nor to the Prophets in the East or the West, nor to Copernicus, nor to Luther, Descartes, or Machiavelli. Judgments of value must henceforth direct technological change, for without such values man is divested of his humanity and of his need to collaborate with the very fabric of the universe in order to bestow meaning, purpose, and dignity upon his existence. No time must be lost since the wavelength of change is now shorter than the life-span of man.

In spite of the infinite obligation of men and in spite of their finite power, in spite of the intransigence of nationalisms, and in spite of the homelessness of moral passions rendered ineffectual by the technological outlook, beneath the apparent turmoil and upheaval of the present, and out of the transformations of this dynamic period with the unfolding of a world-consciousness, the purpose of *World Perspectives* is to help quicken the "unshaken heart of well-rounded truth" and interpret the significant elements of the World Age now taking shape out of the core of that undimmed continuity of the creative process which restores man to mankind while deepening and enhancing his communion with the universe.

RUTH NANDA ANSHEN

For all my students
at the first spring of Lindisfarne

Books by the same author

EVIL AND WORLD ORDER

I

Meditation on the Dark Ages,
Past and Present

All forms hold energy against the flow of time. Spread the energy of a sun equitably throughout space, and you will subtract a star from the heavens. Gather up the galactic dust of space in a spiral, and you can compress the dust into a sun. Expansion and contraction, expression and compression: so the universe goes. Once it was a single atom that began to expand in an explosion; and now it will continue to expand until it reaches the ultimate limit of entropy. With the energies of the aboriginal cosmic atom spread equitably throughout space, it will all be over in the heat-death of the universe. It is only a matter of time, or, rather, *the* matter of time. From hot to cold, from order to disorder, from creation to entropy: over it all the Second Law keeps watch, and black holes compost the light of gravity-collapsing stars.

Modern optimists like Buckminster Fuller like to speak of "synergy," as if there were some magical form that could hold out against the laws of thermodynamics. Surrounded by the signs of an impending tragedy, the collapse of his whole industrial civilization, the liberal optimist refuses to believe in tragedies any more: the past was tragic because they did not have computers in those days. Liberals like Zbigniew Brzezinski and Herman Kahn believe we can eliminate the tragic flaw in man; following Brzezinski, we can replace the chaos of politics with the systems of management; following Kahn, we can hook up the brain to computers to create an electronic superman.[1]* In the science-fiction vision of Arthur C. Clarke, the ultimate society of the future will be programmed by a giant computer, and politics, economics, art, and entertainment will be taken care of in a domed city whose magic circle keeps out chaos and old night.[2]

Although that miracle seems far off, Buckminster Fuller is still reaching out for it and has already drawn a sketch of a dome over Manhattan. For men like Fuller, Brzezinski, and Kahn, tragedy is inconceivable. Their faith in progress is so unthinking that they cannot help but believe that some technological miracle will deliver us at the last dramatic moment. Though we have not been reared on myth, we have all been raised on movies and believe that just as all seems lost and the savages are about to burn the circle of covered wagons, the cavalry will charge in with a joyous noise of bugles and salvation.

The Greeks knew better. Anaximander presided over the case in 560 B.C. and delivered the following judgment:

> The Non-limited is the original material of existing things; further, the source from which existing things derive their existence is also that to which they return at their destruction, according to necessity; for they give justice and make reparation to one another for their injustice, according to the arrangement of Time.[3]

They make reparation for the sin of their existence, for the breaking up of the One into the many. The pieces of the One are things, and things are what man holds onto to maintain the vanity of his own existence.

And before Anaximander, Homer knew better. When the Achaeans invade Troy, they build a wall upon the shore where their ships are beached. Nature builds permeable mem-

*Notes begin on page 112.

branes, but only man is vain enough to build a wall. Behind
that human form set between the opposites of sea and land,
man holds out for a while. But after that while, the forces of
erosion wear it down, and all that bright armor is tumbled
into mud.

> So within the shelter the warlike son of Menoitos
> tended the stricken Eurypylos, and meanwhile the Argives
> and Trojans fought on in massed battle, nor was the Danaans'
> ditch going to hold them back nor the wide wall above it
> they had built for the sake of their ships, and driven a deep
> ditch
> about it, and had not given to the gods grand sacrifices
> so that it might guard their running ships and their masses
> of spoil within it. It had been built in despite of the immortal
> gods, and therefore it was not to stand firm for a long time.
> So long as Hektor was still alive, and Achilleus was angry,
> so long as the citadel of Lord Priam was a city untaken,
> for this time the great wall of the Achaians stood firm. But
> afterwards
> when all the bravest among the Trojans had died in the
> fighting,
> and many of the the Argives gone in their ships to the beloved
> land of their fathers,
> then at last Poseidon and Apollo took counsel
> to wreck the wall, letting loose the strength of rivers upon it,
> all the rivers that run to the sea from the mountains of Ida,
> Rhesos and Heptaporos, Karesos and Rhodios,
> Grenikos and Aisepos, and immortal Skamandros,
> and Simoeis, where much ox-hide armour and helmets were
> tumbled
> in the river mud, and many of the race of the half-god mortals.
> Phoibos Apollo turned the mouths of these waters together
> and nine days long threw the flood against the wall, and Zeus
> rained
> incessantly, to break the wall faster and wash it seaward.

> And the shaker of the earth himself holding in his hands the
>   trident
> guided them, and hurled into the waves all the bastions'
>   strengthening
> of logs and stones the toiling Achaians had set in position
> and made all smooth again by the hard-running passage of
>   Helle
> and once again piled the great beach under sand, having
>   wrecked
> the wall, and turned the rivers again to make the way down
> the same channel where before they had run the bright stream
>   of their water.[4]

As long as Achilles is angry, the war goes on. As long as passion is attached to form, the conflict rages.

Beneath us is the molten core of earth, above us is the burning radiation of the solar wind. Behind the wall of the earth's magnetic field, we keep ourselves together until those apocalyptic times when the poles reverse themselves and every valley is exalted and every hill made plain.

Whether it is the thin film of the biosphere or the thin wall of the Achaeans, man lives at an interface between opposites: earth and sky, sea and shore, life and death. Yet it is precisely the interface between opposites that is the place of transformation, and the energy of that transformation comes from remaining poised at the perilous edge; a slight movement to either side brings dissolution into uniformity.

We live at an interface between order and disorder, and cannot move into one singly without destroying the disequilibrium that is basic to change and evolution. Order and disorder, energy and transformation: it seems almost molecular. Put enough energy into the lattice, and the metal will turn into a gas; slow down the volatile gas, and you can have metal to outlast an aeon. Once again, the Greeks seem to have understood the nature of the choice. In Thucydides's *Peloponnesian War,* the choice is dramatized in the conflict between Sparta and Athens. Be like Sparta and you can live with your highly ordered, barrack-like institutions intact for eight hundred years; be like Athens and you can create everything we know as Greek culture and burn out in ninety years. It is a choice between a Spartan death in life or an Athenian life in death. And the choice is all a matter of values.

How does one hold onto values in an age of the collapse of values? How does one create forms in an age when all forms are coming apart? Like the wall of the Achaeans, our industrial civilization has been built in despite of the gods and now the forces of nature are wearing away at it. But this is not the first time individuals have had to live on while the light of their civilization sputtered.

Like the sixth century A.D., the sixth century B.C. was an age of darkness. The civilizational waves of Sumer and Egypt were receding; whatever was left of the original cultures was lost in the mud and shallows of militaristic states. R. M. Adams has shown that in the evolution of urban society in Mesopotamia and Mesoamerica, cultures began as theocracies, became militaristic polities, and ended up as conquest states.[5] Another way of looking at this evolutionary process is to see that a culture begins in an explosion of myth, a sacred image of nature, self, and society that unites all men in a common dream, and then slowly the forces of routinization take over and the dream begins to fade. The prophet becomes a priest; the shepherd-king becomes a pharaonic Solomon. As the forces of palace, marketplace, and army develop, the myth decays until nothing holds man together but brute force. The disintegrating polity is finally compressed into the militaristic fascist state. Since every state organized for conquest also organizes its enemies to conquer it, such militarism creates the dismal cycle which leads to the destruction of civilization.

According to tradition, Pythagoras was carried away from Egypt to Babylon by the conquering armies of Cambyses. One can picture the historical landscape against which the sage moved: nothing left of the civilization of either Egypt or Babylon, only a recent memory of the unending movement of armies—Hebrew, Assyrian, Persian, and the Mede. The light of civilization that had flamed up in the fourth millennium B.C. was going out, but in the dim light the shadows threw into greater relief the very weakness of that form of human culture.

Civilization had been based upon writing, on the break-up of the unity of the tribe into the literate and the illiterate. It had been based upon urbanization, on standing monuments and standing armies, and, ultimately, upon slavery. The polarities of the age of civilization were the center and the periphery, the temple of the priest and the desert of the prophet. As the centers had decayed, the pastoral vision of the eternal desert had been expressed by Abraham, Moses, and Amos. Then in the sixth century B.C. a new wave of prophecy arose and addressed itself not merely to the moral decay of one center, but to the moral decay of the very idea of civilization itself. Across the world, from Italy to China, a new race of prophets confronted the contradictions of civilization. The vision of the prophets was one of universal religions. It was not a validation of one's own tribal god, for that too easily could grow into the civil religion of a conquest state; it was a vision of the aboriginal brotherhood of man that stood before the walls and battlements of civilization had been raised.

The sixth century B.C. is one of the darkest and the brightest periods in history; it is the age of the Second Isaiah, Jeremiah, and Daniel, of Pythagoras and Zoroaster, of Buddha, Lao-tzu, and Confucius. Why did they all come at the same time? A Jungian would invoke the collective unconscious of the race, a Hopi would speak of the kachinas from other worlds who supervise our evolutionary development, and a Christian poet would answer:

Because the Holy Ghost over the bent
World broods with warm breast and with ah! bright wings.

Let us indulge in a Pynchonesque paranoid fantasy to imagine that the prophets of the sixth century are part of one universal conspiracy. Religion is, after all, supposed to be a subversive conspiracy, "For we wrestle not against flesh and blood, but against principalities, against powers, against the rulers of the darkness of this world, against spiritual wickedness in high places."[6] Certainly the conspiracy theory of history would explain what Pythagoras and Zoroaster were doing together in Persia.[7]

From Egypt and Mesopotamia, Pythagoras took his experience of the mystery schools to the western lands of Magna Graecia in Italy to establish something new, not a hierophantic mystery school for temple initiates, but a secular school for the leaders of society. In short, Pythagoras built the first university and laid the foundations in mathematics, music, and physics for the science upon which Western Civilization is built.

Marshall McLuhan has described the process of change as one in which the sloughed-off environment becomes a work of art in the new invisible environment.[8] This is one way to present the Hegelian dialectic of historical growth. A visual image of the process of *aufheben* is the spiral: we turn back to the past, reconstitute it, and then turn away from it in a new direction. The strategy of change for Pythagoras was to make a synthesis of the religion and science of the dying Near Eastern civilizations, and then miniaturize them as a work of art in the new and still invisible environment of Western Civilization. The old culture became a curriculum in the new culture. In terms of paleontology, this kind of evolutionary change is an example of the principle of Romer's Rule: "The initial survival value of a favorable innovation is conservative, in that it renders possible the maintenance of a traditional way of life in the face of changed circumstances."[9]

At the time of Pythagoras, the Egyptian mystery schools were no longer forces of culture and civilization-building; they were probably priestly bureaucracies subsidized by the state to pass on harmless traditions by rote. The only way to recreate the original purpose of the mystery school was to do something radical, radically conservative. And so Pythagoras created the secular school, the university. As civilization was moving toward entropy, he created a new form to hold old values against the flow of time.

The tragic background against which the school of Pythagoras at Crotona was figured continued, however, to its end. Many were accepted into the Pythagorean discipline, but some were rejected as morally unfit. One of the rejected students is reputed to have raised a rebellion against the influence of the school. In the conflict, the school was burnt to the ground. The Pythagoreans fled throughout Greece, but in their flight, they took the message to the Greek world. Like the seed-pod exploding in its death, the school created new lives, and one of those lives was Plato and his Academy.

Plato's Academy lasted from 385 B.C. to A.D. 529; it became the archetype for all the universities that followed. Pythagoras's school at Crotona lasted for only twenty years. The Pythagorean tradition went underground, but like an underground spring it flowed beneath the foundations of many of the schools that came after. Iamblichus in Syria, Ficino in Florence, Copernicus in Frauenburg, Bruno in Nola, and Heisenberg in Munich: all identified themselves as Pythagoreans. Pythagoras may have died as an old man in exile and despair at the destruction of his life's work, but the success of his short-lived experiment rivals the success of institutions that endured for centuries.

The Pythagorean school at Crotona and the Platonic Academy in Athens exemplify two different ways to hold values against the forces of disorder. One form is the cultural strategy, the other is the permanent institution. One short-lived strategy that affected the life of British civilization, with such longer-lived institutions as Canterbury, Oxford, and Cambridge, was the monastery school of Lindisfarne. Founded in 634 on Holy Island off the coast of Northumbria,

Lindisfarne was another attempt to create light in an age of darkness.

Once again, the sloughed-off environment became a work of art in the new invisible environment. The old Greco-Roman civilization became a curriculum in the new invisible environment of Christian civilization. The school at Crotona was not an Egyptian mystery school, and the monastery school at Lindisfarne was not a Roman Catholic church, but an Irish one. The Roman Church was based upon the imperial model; each city contained a bishop who was answerable to the bishop of bishops in the mother of cities, in Rome. There were no cities in ancient Ireland and Scotland, and so the monastery was set in a totally different culture. The abbot of a monastery was no prince of the church, but a common priest. The Irish Church was no outpost of an imperial ecclesiastical Roman legion, but the continuation of archaic religious forms derived from pagan Ireland and syncretistic Egypt. If according to Romer's Rule every innovation is conservative, it is easy to see that the innovations of the Celtic Church enabled some of the old mystical traditions of archaic Ireland to live on under changed historical circumstances. As Pythagoras had outmystified the hierophants of the mystery schools of Egypt, so St. Columba outdruided the druids.[10] In each case, the innovator was more in the spirit of the tradition than the traditionalists.

The Celtic Church identified itself as the mystical Church of John and not the temporal Church of Peter, and until the Synod of Whitby in 664, which was to shift the influence away from the Celtic to the Roman Church, Lindisfarne was the voice of Christianity in England. With the monastery school as their base, the great saints Aidan and Cuthbert went forth to convert pagan England. In less than thirty years, the work was done. After the defeat of the Synod of Whitby, the Irish monks under Colman went back to Iona from Lindisfarne. Though some monks stayed behind, the great age of Lindisfarne was over. At the turn of the eighth century, the Lindisfarne Gospels were illuminated in memory of Cuthbert, but even great art could not defend the vision. A few years later, Lindisfarne was overrun by the Danes and burnt to the ground.

The burning of Lindisfarne, like the burning of the school at Crotona, reveals that many of these efforts to create light are figured against intensely dark backgrounds. In modern times, the Bauhaus seems to be a pre-eminent example of a cultural force arising at the same time that the opposite forces of Nazism were growing all around it. And once again, it was the very dissolution of the Bauhaus that carried its energies to London and Chicago.[11]

What we can learn from Crotona, Lindisfarne, or the Bauhaus is that a small and short-lived community can serve as a catalytic enzyme to effect a change in the entire organism of a civilization, and that sometimes these changes are as important as the more obvious contributions of permanent institutions. Institutions are appropriate structures for the continuation of a tradition, but they are not appropriate forms for the creation of the new or the revitalization of the old.

The other principle we can learn from Crotona and Lindisfarne is the necessity of conserving a civilization by intensifying it through miniaturization. Pythagoras miniaturized the Near Eastern civilization; the Irish monks miniaturized Greco-Roman civilization; now we need to miniaturize industrial civilization.

The sloughed-off environment is industrial civilization; the invisible environment is what Teilhard de Chardin called "the Planetization of Mankind."[12] To turn industrial civilization into a work of art in this still invisible environment, we must not only miniaturize our factories, we must also miniaturize the great universal religions which created the basis of internationalism. The universal religions were created in response to the contradictions of civilization, but we are no longer living in civilization. The polarities between elitist center and provincial periphery have been overcome by modern communications and spiritual consciousness. Planetary culture is not the international civilization of London, Paris, Tokyo, and New York; it is a new consciousness in which "The center is everywhere and the circumference nowhere." The universal religions were the precursors of planetary culture, but now that we are moving from civilization to planetization, we need to take up (aufheben) these religions and miniaturize them in a curriculum for a new culture.

If we are going to humanize a technology that now contains thermonuclear warfare, ecological destruction, and such subtler destructions as psychosurgery, electrical stimulation of the brain, aversive therapy, and behavioral modification, we will need more than the liberal humanism expressed in the implicit system of values of the behavioral sciences and the traditional humanities. The world view of the liberal intellectual is a Marxist-Freudian mapping of the outer world of society and the inner world of the psyche; but that sophisticated world view does not contain the celestial and cthonic energies we need to appreciate the machine for what it is worth. To see technology in proper scale, we need cosmic consciousness, and that consciousness comes more often from meditation than from reading Marx or Freud.

If we cannot humanize our technology with liberal humanism, we can with animism. And that is the importance to the contemporary world of animistic communities like Findhorn.[13] If we can converse with plants, hear the spirits of wind and water, and listen to the molecular chorus singing the ninety-nine names of God in the crystal lattice of the metal of our machines, then we can have the consciousness we need to live in a culture in harmony with the universe.

In an unconscious fashion, man has already begun to shift away from materialism to information, and the giantism of the machines he once worshiped is giving way to tiny circuitry. If the space program sent off rockets to the moon that were taller than skyscrapers, it spun off to earth machines in which millions of electrons danced on the head of a pin. As our entire technology becomes as miniaturized as our hand-held calculators and desk-top computers, the whole scale of the human body to technology changes. Like paleolithic hunters of the Solutrean culture, whose tools were pieces of sculpture in their hands, we will hold our technology and not be held by it.

As the scale of man to machine changes, so does the scale of the individual to institutions. In an electronic technology, one need not drive to a Berkeley type university to watch a lecture on a television console with four hundred other students; he can stay home to watch the Berkeley university program on cable television, and if he doesn't like Berkeley, he can switch the channel to Harvard or Oxford. As more students stay home, and as more information is carried on cable, the university will no longer have to sustain a huge complex of buildings. The university will grow smaller as it grows larger and the university will be everywhere and the campus nowhere.

As more and more information is carried into the home, the individual will experience a need for new groupings. On the turn of the spiral, man will return to the tribal forms of the hunters and gatherers, and in these societies, "The magic numbers are 25 and 500."[14] As the individual moves out of the environment of the institution, a symbolic environment in which he gains his information through the reading of buildings and books, he moves into the larger environment of the Noosphere, a vibratory environment he experiences through meditation, ritual chanting, and dance. As the cosmic environment expands in the Noosphere, the human community compensatorily contracts into the hunting band of 25 or the meta-industrial planetary village of 500.

As one moves from the institutions of civilization in church, university, and capital-intensive factory into the new planetary villages, he moves into a religion without priests, a university without professors, and manufacture without factories. The factory mass-produces cheap goods with built-in obsolescence, but in an era of scarcity of materials in which "The Limits to Growth" are envisaged, we will no longer be able to afford the waste of energy and materials contained in the mass production of cheap goods. Of necessity, we will have to return to the medieval craft-guild workshop. Since the goods will have to be crafted to last a lifetime, they will have to be built with a Zen mindfulness to every detail, and so the labor-intensive workshop will contain, not an army of workers, but a mystery guild of contemplatives. Like the furniture of the Shakers, the goods of the planetary village will be very good indeed.[15]

In a labor-intensive community of contemplatives, more is done with less capital, so money is surrounded, compressed, and miniaturized by a culture not based upon greed. As inflation prices industrial civilization out of existence, communities of caring and sharing are brought into being and families are forced into finding other means than money to structure their lives. In a culture of Buddhist "Right Livelihood," money is not eliminated, any more than technology; both are miniaturized. The Buddhist tone of "Right Livelihood" may sound foreign to the American Way, but, interestingly enough, just such a political economy was envisioned by Jefferson. In words that ring out as a startling prophecy of our contemporary fascination with decentralized China, Jefferson wrote to van Hogendorp in 1785:

> You ask what I think on the expediency of encouraging our States to be commercial? Were I to indulge my own theory, I should wish them to practise neither commerce nor navigation, but to stand, with respect to Europe, precisely on the footing of China.[16]

As the Church lost the vision of its founder, so has the country lost the vision of its founding fathers, but now that industrial society is strangling in its own contradictions, we have one last chance to re-vision human society.

"The Protestant Ethic and the Spirit of Capitalism" spurred the growth of industrial civilization, so it is natural to assume that the growth of planetary culture is being spurred by a new spiritual sensibility. Side by side with the miniaturization of technology, we are also experiencing the miniaturization of religion, and just about every esoteric school is now opening itself to the new global culture of our technological society. Yoga, Sufism, Tibetan and Zen Buddhism, Yaqui shamanism, and Celtic animism. the planet has become a Ptolemaic Egypt of syncretistic religious movements, and the Alexandria of it all is America. And this is no accident, for all these esoteric techniques have what we need to transform our exoteric technologies. Europe and Asia groan under the burden of their own past greatness, but America is still the place where all the cultures of the world can come together in consummation of the past and realization of the future.

At the contemporary Lindisfarne in America, we have tried to turn the old culture into a new curriculum. We have neither guru and disciples nor church and worshipers, but we do have a spiritual fellowship in which men and women serve as teaching fellows in Yoga, Buddhism, Sufism, Esoteric Christianity, and Mystical Judaism. In a college, the curriculum is based upon the Great Books of Western Civilization, but at Lindisfarne the curriculum is based upon the Great Techniques for the transformation of consciousness. Lindisfarne's scientists, artists, and scholars have one thing in common: their lives are rooted in one of the great contemplative paths of transformation. As the school at Crotona was not a mystery school, and as the monastery at Lindisfarne was not a Roman Catholic church, so we are not a simple continuation of the past. We *have* a farm, but *are* not a farm; we have children in the community, but we are not a private school; we have postdoctoral fellows, but are not a think tank; we have retired people, but we are not a retirement community; and we have yogis, but we are not an ashram. We have gone back on the spiral to the preindustrial community to create, on a higher plane with the most advanced scientific and spiritual thought we can achieve, the planetary, meta-industrial village. We have moved in consciousness out of the large nation-state into the even larger planet; we have moved out in body from the city to the smaller multigenerational community. With the "Buddhist economics" of E. F. Schumacher of London, the technological thought of the New Alchemists of Woods Hole, the agriculture of Findhorn, the scientific philosophy of Whitehead, and the religious thought of Sri Aurobindo and Teilhard de Chardin, we are trying to create an educational community that can become a mutational deme in which cultural evolution can move from civilization to planetization.

In the nineteenth century the polarities of culture were the romantic artist and the industrial engineer. Then Shelley could say that "Poets are the unacknowledged legislators of the world." But now that is no longer true. In the shift from civilization to planetization it is the mystic who has become the unacknowledged legislator of the world: a Sri Aurobindo or a Teilhard de Chardin, and not a Norman Mailer or an Andy Warhol. The artist cannot save civilization, and in the search for form it is not the artist who will discover and create the new culture. We have lived long enough with the myth of The Artist, and now that the paintings decorate banks and the poems lead to suicide, it is time to move on and let the artist remain behind, whimpering in the corners of his ego.[17]

In abandoning The Artist we will not lose the beautiful, we will regain the beauty the artist lost sight of. Pythagoras, Columba, Quetzalcoatl: the builders of cultures were themselves versed in the arts of civilization and could provide the myths that would sustain new artists for generations.

Art is dead. Science is dead.[18] Now even the Pope is willing to say that "It seems the Church is destined to die."[19] Our entire civilization is dying. But what is death? Consider the yogi: when he stops his heart consciously, he is dead by technical definition, but actually he is reborn, for in taking the energy out of the cardiovascular into the central nervous system, he experiences ecstasy and enlightenment. He does not die, he dances his death. So now we need to dance out the death of industrial civilization and experience, not its painful, apocalyptic destruction, but its joyous, millennial destructuring. And if we cannot, then we will not create our destiny, but be forced to endure our fate.

II

We Become What We Hate

Thoughts can become inverted when they are reflected in actions.

The doctor who thought he was inventing a pill to help women become pregnant was actually inventing the Pill. The existential psychologists who created the "Third Movement" as a counter to Freudian and behavioral psychology thought they were creating new forms for the transformation of the self; actually they were creating new forms for the elimination of the self. Now your emotions belong to your corporation and you must be free and open in T-groups and management sensitivity-training sessions. And when you are home alone with your wife, you can experience her through the "Marriage Enrichment Program" kit offered for $29.95 by the existential psychologists who work for Bell & Howell Human Development Corporation.

If the learned psychologists did not know what they were doing in the "Third Movement," we should expect that the creators of most social movements and revolutions have no idea of what the outcome of their thoughts will be. The California educators who thought that they were extending civilization and heightening democracy through universal higher education were actually creating Youth Culture.

And even the hippies lacked foresight. In the summer of 1967 they thought they were social radicals, but they were really only the R & D wing of American advertising at work on leisure and consumer behavior in a fully automated society. The hippies tried to move as far out as they could, but it took Madison Avenue only two years to catch up.

Cultural revolutionaries like Dr. Ivan Illich thought that they were being far-out when they proposed "Deschooling Society," but they were actually only about four years ahead of President Nixon. Dr. Illich thought he was creating "alternatives in education" for the preindustrial Third World, but he was actually designing postinstitutional forms of learning for the meta-industrial world.

The public school is vanishing with middle-class industrial society. Now the blacks want to take their children away from white teachers and tranquilizers, the suburban whites want to take their children away from inner-city blacks, and the intellectuals want to take their children out of institutional training.

And since all this is going on in a media society that makes the old institutions redundant, the pseudo environment of the school is being overwhelmed by the true environment. With technological saturation pulling to the left, and economic recession pulling to the right, the base for our present expensive state socialist educational system is being pulled apart. Now that schools and universities are merely middle-class public service corporations, minorities of the left and right and dissident intellectuals will have to go elsewhere for the life of the mind and soul. As they try to escape state socialism, they will be attracted to Dr. Illich's anarchist capitalism, until finally the government itself will give in and switch to the voucher system. Dr. Illich thought he was a radical, but he was merely the R & D wing of HEW.

Radicals are not the only ones who misperceive the outcome of their thoughts. President Nixon thought that in moving to create an all-volunteer army he was moving to demilitarize the country; actually he was completing the transformation of America into a banana republic. Professional soldiers have little difficulty in firing on civilian crowds, and army juntas have even less difficulty in taking governments away from the effete "pinkos" who lack the *cojones* to do their own fighting. And so we encounter the paradox: Dr. Illich, in trying to be radical, became truly conservative; President Nixon, in trying to be conservative, became truly radical.

But there are even greater paradoxes in history than these. We are supposed to be a spiritual, God-fearing nation in conflict with the Godless materialism of the Communist countries. And yet Mao's China is built on self-sacrifice, hard work, frugality, Benedictine poverty, ecological respect for nature, and deep belief in the power of meditation on the thought of Mao. In Mao's Mary Baker Eddy version of Marxist dialectical materialism, if one has right thinking he does not need machines. Mao thinks he is creating a religionless society, but really he has created the largest Puritan state in the history of mankind. We think we are the inheritors of Plimoth Plantation, but actually we are the decadent Europe that the Pilgrims tried to leave behind.

What these paradoxes of opposites are all about is a phenomenology in which it is part of the very nature of passionate conflict to turn one into his own enemy. "We become what we hate" is an old yoga maxim. And in watching the conflict of the Irish Troubles, the Dublin yogi, George William Russell ("A.E."), developed the maxim into a principle of political science: "By intensity of hatred nations create in themselves the characters they imagine in their enemies. Hence it is that all passionate conflicts result in the interchange of characteristics."

If one stops to consider the implications of this principle for the conflicts of the Second World War, he will come to some disquieting conclusions. Japan is now Los Angeles and Detroit, and Big Sur, California, is a Zen Mountain Center. Germany is now a consumer society, and we are the largest militarist state in the history of the world. We have become our enemy.

III

Three Wise Men of Gotham

One comes away from the book *Technological Change* as from a scholarly conference: with an ever renewed amazement that so formidable an activity can accomplish so little. Emmanuel Mesthene's book could very well be a transcript of the chairman's remarks from such a conference, for it is full of the usual ploys: the framing of large questions that are left unanswered, the calls for more research, the name-dropping that shows little insight into the authors mentioned, the plugs for one's own university department and program. Here is a book published with the Harvard brand name, but it amounts to little more than a commercial for the Harvard University Program on Technology and Society. With its eighty-nine pages of text set in very large type, this essay simply does not merit publication in any form other than mimeograph distribution to the members of the Harvard Program; but since IBM is supporting the Program, so unprestigious an expression cannot be countenanced, and so the work is shoved in our faces.

Nowhere is the banality of technocratic liberalism so compactly expressed as in this bloated pamphlet. "With the proper economic and political organization, we could derive greater benefits from our technology than we do" represents the extent of the work's contribution to existing knowledge. So much like a conference chairman, Professor Mesthene asks a few important questions, but drops them because they are too large, and other members of the Harvard Program are at work on them. We are to trust that the amount of scholarly production coming from the Program will convince IBM to continue its support so that the answers will come pouring out in a whole series of Harvard monographs on Technology and Society.

How is it that Harvard of all places can be so stupid? Why is it that for all the work of the New Left, Old Right, and Red Tories the banalities of technocratic liberalism glide smoothly over the cracking surface of American society. In works like Mesthene's and other Cambridge products like the "Daedalus" project on the year 2000, one can only surmise that Cambridge, U.S.A., is the capital of technocratic liberalism, and that those in the capital are always the last to find out. Professor Mesthene is supposed to be a specialist in Technology and Society, and although he drops some names on page 23, he shows himself to be totally ignorant of the ideas and implications of the work of Ellul, Mumford, Marcuse, C. S. Lewis, Noam Chomsky, Ivan Illich, and George Grant. How is it after all that has been written in studies and screamed in the streets an expert can write such sentences:

> Technology, as I have noted, creates new possibilities for human choice and action, but leaves their disposition uncertain. What its effects will be and what ends it will serve are not inherent in the technology but depend on what man will do with technology.[1]

The cliché is vapidly reasserted that technology is only a tool to be used for good or ill, as the user chooses; and since technology gives the user a choice that he didn't have before, it really is positively good while it is scrupulously neutral. Since more distinguished writers have challenged this assumption, I should probably not rise to the bait, but one more time.

Technology is not a tool, it is a culture. As an environment of symbols whose most important expressions are not machines and buildings but the institutions they embody, technology is powerful enough to warp even starlight as it passes through its field. When you live in such an environment, you are not free to pick up one tiny tool and use it as you choose. You are overwhelmingly constrained to perform according to the culture of rationalization and the process definition of values. Because the technocrat claims that values are not eternal a priori forms of human consciousness, he is free to bend them to fit the requirements of *his* time. The real thrust of this book, like the real transformation of the new MIT, is the call for a shift from technological hardware to the implementation of whole new managerial-governmental systems for the control of an advanced technological society. And if such traditional values as religion or the Constitution stand in the way, they must be modified in a progressive fashion. Values, as every good liberal knows, are not Platonic forms or "pure categories of the Understanding"; they are constantly changing accommodations to historical change: since man is in process, he can be processed.

II

When Western Man moved from a Christian to a commercial civilization in the Industrial Revolution, he became no longer a loyal subject of the throne and altar, but a citizen. Now that the age of the middle-class industrial nation-states seems to have stopped, and now that another technological revolution seems to be taking off like a multistage rocket, it appears that the era of the citizen is to be left behind, floating with the junk of history. In a period of executively directed government, the individual citizen and his representatives appear unable to deal with government, war, economic disorder, crime, pollution, and cultural decay. In solitary confinement before his color TV, the citizen is made a part of all that is happening on a planetary scale and impressed with his powerlessness to act on precisely that planetary scale. Closed in upon himself, the citizen is not the yeoman structure that creates the content of the Republic, but simply a photograph in a collage enormously larger than himself. And so the cycle of history turns and man has become a loyal subject of pageantries once again, but this time he is subject, not to the throne and altar of Christian civilization, but to the electronic hierophants of the Mysteries of behavioral science.

Professor B. F. Skinner is one of the princes of the church of behavioral science and, as such, one of the foremost linear thinkers of our time. A fervent modernizer who is himself something of a relic of the time of Comte, Fourier, Bentham, and Saint-Simon, Skinner carries on with the nineteenth-century attempt to eliminate traditional human culture in favor of one that is sensible, scientific, and efficient.

It is hard to imagine a world in which people live together without quarreling, maintain themselves by producing the food, shelter, and clothing they need, enjoy themselves and contribute to the enjoyment of others in art, music, literature, and games, consume only a reasonable part of the resources of the world and add as little as possible to its pollution, bear no more children than can be raised decently, continue to explore the world around them and discover better ways of dealing with it, and come to know themselves effectively. Yet all this is possible. . . .[2]

All this is possible if only we follow Professor Skinner to move beyond the Constitution and other literatures of freedom and dignity to the control of human behavior through the scientific design of a culture.

The possibilities have been glimpsed before for readers familiar with Skinner's novel, *Walden Two,* and so one expects this latest book to contain refinements and responses to his critics. But Dr. Skinner does not like criticism, and if his critics are as bright as Professor Noam Chomsky, he prefers not to finish reading their painstakingly devastating critiques. He can quote C. S. Lewis's *The Abolition of Man,* an intelligent refutation of behavioral engineering, and then go on with his old argument to prove only that he simply cannot take in anything that is contrary to his *idée fixe*.

Human beings are social creatures; they live in cultures, listen to one another, and change from the persuasion and touches of friends and enemies. But Dr. Skinner does not like to listen or change; he does not like this human culture of ours, and so he is out to eliminate it in favor of one in which no criticism of the behavioral managers is conceivable. Consequently, there is something futile about criticizing a book by Skinner: a man who addresses himself to multitudes he will not hear should be an artist who places himself above the opinions of the crowd; but the man who takes human nature itself to be his material to be twisted into shape is an artist *manqué* in the tradition of Hitler. Skinner himself is harmless; it is the Skinnerites who worry me. Gobineau was a harmless intellectual crank, but out of his harmless theory of the intellectual superiority of the Aryan race came National Socialism. As Keynes noted: "The political fanatic who is hearing voices in the air has distilled his frenzy from the work of some academic scribbler of a few years back."

So since Dr. Skinner will not listen to his critics, I will address myself to his students and possible followers. What if we were to give all power to the behaviorists? The structural processing of information in the human mind is dualistic: light and dark, good and evil, yes and no, this or that, 1 or 0. *It follows then, that any social rule, implicit or explicit, is set in consciousness so that its negative inversion automatically comes into existence with its positive formulation.* If you say, "Love Big Brother," you are setting up the syntax to say, preconsciously, "Do not love Big Brother." If you say, "Behave nicely," you are bringing into consciousness the possibility of its opposite. All human thoughts come into the mirror as they become reflected in consciousness; the subconscious is, therefore, not so much Freud's jungle of repressed desires as it is the mirror-image of a particular culture. Any society, behavioral or Baptist, is therefore going to contain the negation of itself *if the people are conscious*. Consequently, the very structures of behavioral design in *Walden Two* are the very things which will bring the community into conflict—which is a realization that all dialectical thinkers from Heraclitus to Kolakowski have emphasized. Everything contains its contradiction.

Conflict is, therefore, not simply an expression of the cultural environment as Skinner would have us believe. Conflict is the expression of the tragic necessity in which the contradiction must exist if its positive is to be. In the binary world, man knows by twos: joy and suffering, freedom and tyranny, birth and death, good and evil. Put a *man* in a behavioral utopia and he is still a man *thinking* in terms of 1–0, kiss–kill, love–hate. Only by altering the very structure of consciousness can conflict be eliminated, but to effect that alteration, we would have to eliminate the mind. People who could never turn structures inside out, think in mirror-images, dream up Marxist contradictions, and deal in the values of positive and negatives would be literally mindless. Thus in order to perfect man, science would have to create a society in which no science was possible. The scientific controllers would, therefore, have to be outside the controls by which they ruled the fixed human beings; and since, as Skinner says, "the relations between the controller and the controlled are reciprocal," human nature would break in half and supermen would rule androids. But if the behavioral controls are created to protect man from the evil and conflict of the old days of civilization, and if the controllers are outside these controls so as to preserve their scientific powers of reasoning, then the controllers will be unprotected from evil and will come into conflict with one another; and so inevitably the caste of psychologist-kings will destroy itself.

If Skinner wanted to be absolutely consistent, he should have followed Arthur C. Clarke's science-fiction novel *The City and the Stars*, in which men are entrusted to the rule of a gigantic computer. If the behavioral scientists could design machines to keep man alive and happy in cultural containers filled with the dead arts of a once living mankind, and then throw the switch that would subject themselves as well to the rule of the machine, perhaps mankind would finally be able to move beyond the agony of existence. But then he would be, like some ancient Pharaoh surrounded by all the trappings of his former high culture, simply equipped for life in his tomb.

So no matter how one looks at it, Skinner's designs on human culture can never work. The dialectical problems of human consciousness cannot be solved in the terms of a linear behavioral technology. The technologist like Dr. Skinner is simply a flashlight in search of the nature of darkness: the more he looks for it, the more he chases it away.

III

Culture should always surround technology, but in the case of Dr. Skinner, technology is surrounding culture. With the work of Dr. José M. Delgado, the surrounding of technology becomes quite literal as the brain is encircled by a cyclone fence of electrodes.

> Electrodes were implanted in her right temporal lobe and upon stimulation of a contact located in the superior part about thirty millimeters below the surface, the patient reported a pleasant tingling sensation in the left side of her body "from my face down to the bottom of my legs." She started giggling and making funny comments, stating that she enjoyed the sensation "very much." Repetition of these stimulations made the patient more communicative and flirtatious, and she ended by openly expressing her desire to marry the therapist. . . . The second patient openly expressed her fondness for the therapist (who was new to her), kissed his hands, and talked about her immense gratitude for what was being done for her.[3]

It would seem that Frazier in *Walden Two* knew what he was about when he said: "What is love, except another name for the use of positive reinforcement?" Delgado's research makes even Orwell's *1984* seem out of date, for there torture was used to retrain the disturbed to love Big Brother. If Delgado's assumptions are correct, then the Future State can replace control through torture with control through pleasure:

> A systematic analysis of the neuroanatomical distribution of pleasurable areas in the rat (164) shows that 60 percent of the brain is neutral, 35 percent is rewarding, and only 5 percent may elicit punishing effects. The idea that far more brain is involved in pleasure than in suffering is rather optimistic and gives hope that this predominance of the potential for pleasurable sensations can be developed into a more effective behavioral reality.[4]

If more of the brain, rat or human, is involved in pleasure, then it seems likely that future behavioral managers will reason that it is absurdly wasteful to create a political technology based upon pain, force, and terror. Perhaps the managers will feel that aversive therapy is counterproductive in public relations, but that a "convertive-affective therapy is humane to the subject and positive in terms of its feedback to the clinicians." If a therapist of the near future were ever to encounter an extremely disturbed, highly resistant, antisocial personality, it would be much easier to convert him through extreme pleasure than through pain. It is also highly doubtful that most character formations could stand up under the sweet burden of intense and protracted pleasure. If the momentary "total body orgasm" experienced when a drug addict injects Methedrine is sufficient to alter the personality, then it is obvious that a total body orgasm protracted over a period of hours or days would be sufficient to alter a person's perception of time, his perception of his own life history, and the self-image and character structure derived from these. From the point of view of the behavioral scientist, this would be pleasant work in what could be amiable surroundings. If we now use toys and cartoon murals in pediatric offices and clinics, then the social clinic of the technological society would not have to look like a laboratory at all; instead, it could look like the interior of *Playboy* magazine.

Dr. Delgado's main purpose in his research is, of course, not to create salons of pleasure, but to discover cures for epileptic and brain-damaged persons who suffer from seizures of uncontrollable violence. In this he has been successful and is deserving of the modest fame he now enjoys. But like most human beings, Dr. Delgado is a contradictory creature. At one moment he is pooh-poohing naïve fantasies of a race of robots with radios implanted in their brains by the CIA, but at the next he is telling us how we now can move "toward a psychocivilized society" by "conquering the mind." One side of the profile of Dr. Delgado is the smiling, reassuring, deeply humanistic and widely read family physician; the other side shows the Faustian gleam of the laboratory technician.

> The chronicle of human civilization is the story of a cooperative venture consistently marred by self-destruction, and every advance has been accompanied by increased efficiency of violent behavior. . . .
>
> Ours is a tragically imbalanced industrial society which devotes most of its resources to the acquisition of destructive power and invests insignificant effort in the search which would provide the true weapons of self-defense: knowledge of the mechanisms responsible for violent behavior. They are necessarily related with intracerebral processes of neuronal activity, even if the triggering causality may reside in environmental circumstances. Violence is a product of cultural environment and is an extreme form of aggression, distinct from modes of self-expression required for survival and development under normal conditions.[5]

Delgado takes issue with the behaviorists, for he is deeply concerned with the contribution of the organism to the stimulus-response mechanism and would define mind as "the intracerebral elaboration of extracerebral information." But it is clear from the above that his disagreement with the behaviorists is only one of degree. Like Skinner, Delgado believes that "violence is a product of the cultural environment." If one does not think in terms of the inherent values of the organism, then there is no convincing argument against manipulation; technology can improve upon biology to eliminate the vestigial ape in man, and cultural design can eliminate the correspondingly primitive institutions. If mind is bestowed upon the organism by culture, and science is the most important institution of that culture, then the physical control of the mind can be presented as, not the destruction of a pre-existing entity, but the creative and scientific improvement of parenthood. In order to justify his science of the brain, it is absolutely essential that Delgado feel that his work is only the last act in man's conquest of nature. The raw organic premind is a jungle waiting to be cleared, developed, and civilized. What man has been able before to do to the environment is now about to be done within the brain.

> The mind is not a static, inborn entity owned by the individual and self-sufficient, but the dynamic organization of sensory perceptions of the external world, correlated and reshaped through the internal anatomical and functional structure of the brain. Personality is not an intangible, immutable way of reacting, but a flexible process in continuous evolution, affected by its medium. . . .[6]

It is quite possible that Delgado is correct when he says that "human beings are born without minds," but one can draw two conclusions from this perception. One leads in the direction of genetic engineering and the physical control of the mind; the other leads in the direction of "the no-mind" of Zen Buddhism. Of course it depends upon what you mean by "mind." Delgado feels that because there are "no detectable signs of mental activity at birth," humans have no minds until they are bestowed by their culture. It follows quite naturally that the more scientific is the culture, the more mind there is to be bestowed upon neonates. However, not all of Delgado's data support his conclusions.

> As the fetus grows, many organs perform something like a dress rehearsal before their functions are really required. This is usually referred to as the principle of anticipatory morphological maturation. The heart starts to beat when there is no blood to pump; the gastrointestinal tract shows peristaltic movements and begins to secrete juices in the absence of food; the eyelids open and close in the eternal darkness of the uterus; the arms and legs move, giving the mother the indescribable joy of feeling a new life inside herself; even breathing movements appear several weeks before the birth when there is no air to breathe.[7]

Why, then, should we not suppose that the brain "thinks" before the culture has given it any thoughts to think? There is, of course, an arbitrary aspect to this: it is much like defining a sound as a vibrating body, a medium, and a receiver. Without a receiver, there is no sound; without a culture, there is no mind. But it is not all arbitrary, for if the organism develops before it encounters its environment, then it meets the environment *on its own terms.*

> Some efferent pathways appear before any afferent fiber enters the cerebrum. Initially, the cerebral association system develops toward the motor system and the peripheral sensory fibers grow toward the receptor field. Significant conclusions from these facts are that "the individual acts on its environment before it reacts to its environment." . . . Total behavior is not made up of reflexes; rather, "the mechanism of the total pattern is an essential component of the performance of the part, i.e., the reflex," and behavior therefore "cannot be fully explained in terms of S-R (stimulus-response)." . . . This reveals that "the cerebral

growth determines the attitude of the individual to its environment before that individual is able to receive any sensory impression of its environment. Hence, the initiative is within the organism."[8]

If Delgado understood the material he quoted, he would have to scrap his whole philosophy of mind. The implications that derive from the observations made by the scientists that Delgado quotes seem to indicate that the organism is like a magnetic field; what is magnetized into the field in terms of sensory inputs is determined by the a priori structure of the organism. Human nature precedes the encounter with environmental nature. Delgado seems unfamiliar with the work of Eric Lenneberg at Harvard and Noam Chomsky at MIT concerning the biologically innate aspects of language ability. Familiarization with this work would help in giving some precise content to Delgado's vague definition of the mind as "the intracerebral elaboration of extracerebral information." Culture can shape the "sensory inputs" of the surface structure of language by determining whether the child is to speak Chinese or English, but it cannot determine the deep structure of language which is the species-specific aspect of language ability. Delgado's ignorance of the research done at Harvard's Center for Cognitive Studies and MIT's Linguistic Acquisition Laboratory seriously weakens his attempts to generalize on the basis of his own limited research. He does not really understand the nature of the argument between behaviorism and rationalism, and his philosophical amateurism allows him to indulge in sloppy and circular definitions: "Behavior is the result of motor activities which range from a simple muscular twitch to the creation of a work of art." Quite content to philosophize in an outdated form of empiricism, Delgado blithely ignores Whitehead's warning that "the order of nature cannot be justified by the mere observation of nature."

Mind is the *content* of consciousness, but not its *structure;*

there is the knower and the known, but what is that consciousness that is neither knower nor known?

> Who is the third who walks always beside you?
> When I count, there are only you and I together
> But when I look ahead up the white road
> There is always another one walking beside you
> Gliding wrapt in a brown mantle, hooded
> I do not know whether a man or a woman
>   But who is that on the other side of you?[9]

The fetus lives in the oceanic feeling of oneness; its body
temperature is matched to that of the amniotic fluid so that
it cannot sense where it ends and the universe begins. In this
primordial state all is one, and since mind is two we can
imagine that the fetus is mindless. Then comes birth, the fall
from unity into multiplicity, and the beginning of twos in the
self and the other. But multiplicity makes a new order possible in the segmental articulation of language, and so we find
the Hegelian dialectic of: (1) Unity, (2) Fragmentation, (3)
Reintegration. But the culture cannot create language any
more than the wind can create sailboats; culture can only
startle the brain into mind.

But a mind is both a blessing and a curse; expression requires suppression. To regain the transcendental sentience in
which the self is continuous with the universe, the verbal adult
has to move out of words into the no-mind of Zen. Recent
research by Dr. Robert Keith Wallace into the physiological
effects of meditation suggests that the meditational state of
consciousness is no mere fantasy of the experiencing subject.[10] And so in growth the dialectic repeats itself: verbal
consciousness becomes Unity, concentration becomes the
Fragmentation of mind, and yogic mastery (samadhi)
becomes the Reintegration. "First there is a mountain, then
there is no mountain, then there is." The oceanic presen-
tience of the fetus and the transcendental sentience of the

yogi or roshi are thus structurally alike in that they exist at the opposite sides of the mind.

Dr. Wallace's research indicates that individuals can be taught to move into meditative states of consciousness and that these deeper states of consciousness can be therapeutic in the treatment of mental and physical diseases. Through mysticism the individual can become what Abraham Maslow called "a self-actualizing personality"; through mechanism the individual can become a physically controlled, psychocivilized subject. The choice is clear; it is only the middle ground that seems treacherously muddy. The humanistic movement that began with the Renaissance has reached its limit, and at that limit Western culture has broken apart as mechanism and mysticism move in opposite directions along the circumference of human civilization. If the opposites are to meet in some completion of the sphere of human culture, I do not think they will meet in the constellation of Delgado. Now as the oceans fill up with mercury, it is time to have done with Western, Faustian Man. The conquest of nature, the conquest of space, and the ultimate conquest of the mind: all these images of conquest only express our old pathologically unbalanced culture. Dr. Delgado assures us that he is against aggression, but his conquering of the mind is aggression raised to another order of magnitude.

"The once sacred rights of man must change in many ways," said H. Bentley Glass upon the occasion of his retirement from the presidency of the American Association for the Advancement of Science. What the good doctor had in mind was compulsory abortion for the unfit, genetic control, and all that sort of thing. At the end of humanism it is the human body that has become the battleground where mechanism and mysticism fight it out toward the year 2000. Marx was prophetic, for impotent man now exposes himself to virile machine—and camera; but all the breasts and genitals of pornography cannot put Homo Sapiens together again. The justice is poetic: the

North Americans who once rolled over the Indians with the railroads of the nineteenth century are now about to be turned into Indians by their own technology; it remains to be seen whether these will be the dejected Indians of the Plains or the elevated Indians of Rishikesh.

IV

Occulture: Out of Sight, Out of Mind

So many holes have been poked in Western Civilization that now that all the hot air is gone and a cold and alien wind is coming in, the civilized elite seem to be drawing deeply into themselves and their old convictions in search of warmth and comfort. In these declining years of the Magnus Annus the most interesting minds seem to have moved on long ago; now only the "intellectuals" are left wrapped in their greatcoats of Europe and dreaming of leftist politics or the "new" creations of the avant-garde; but these are the warm dreams that come charitably to all those who are about to freeze to death. Better to turn and die running in a new direction than to stand still and become an historical monument of ice. If one moves in a new direction, he takes a risk that contains the possibility of survival; there is always the chance that the paths others have taken out of Western Civilization may truly lead to a better place. For an intellectual perhaps the most attractive way out has been created by the anthropologist. As Lévi-Strauss noticed in *Tristes Tropiques:*

> As he moves forward with his environment, Man takes with him all the positions that he has occupied in the past, and all those that he will occupy in the future. He is everywhere at the same time, a crowd which, in the act of moving forward, yet recapitulates at every instant every step that it has ever taken in the past. For we live in several worlds, each more true than the one within it, and each false in relation to that within which it is enveloped.[1]

Intellectuals like Lévi-Strauss are fascinated by primitives, but others may prefer the way out provided by schizophrenics; they would follow the way of R. D. Laing: "The cracked open mind of the schizophrenic can let in a light that cannot penetrate the intact but closed mind of the sane." There are many other ways out: one can follow Piaget into the mind of the child, Carlos Castaneda into the mind of the sorcerer, John Lilly into the mind of the dolphin, or Carl Sagan into the mind of an extraterrestrial being. All the ways lead in different directions, but they all move away from the traditional centers of civilization.

It was ships and new navigational instruments that first led man away from the Old to the New World. Perhaps we should suspect that once again technology is leading us into these new unexplored areas, for there does seem to be a relationship between technological and cultural change. In the first Industrial Revolution the dislocations brought about by new machines and institutions led men back into an artistic celebration of the old feudal world view. Wordsworth's peasant was to an industrial society what Laing's schizophrenic is to our managerial society. Writers from Maria Edgeworth to D. H. Lawrence moved in a counterclockwise direction in response to industrialization, but less literary members of the civilized elite looked for other ways in which to understand the complete transformation of human culture. In feudal culture literature had been the supreme instrument for social analysis, but in the Industrial Revolution new forms of knowledge were developed to deal with the problems of cultural change. From the political economy of Smith and Ricardo to the sociology of Engels, Marx, Durkheim, and Weber, the "disenchantment" with European Civilization generated new ways of knowing what man was all about. Of course, for feudal, sophisticated, and literate members of the elite, these new forms were highly suspect.

Now that we are in "The Second Industrial Revolution," it is not surprising that new forms of knowledge are being generated; and it seems that nonfiction is displacing the traditional literary forms. When the planet is being transformed, we want news about the planetary happening, not a novel about a day in the life of a neurotic artist. The novel is basically the autobiography of the middle classes; it is the story of their movement from rags to riches. That is all well and good when there are interesting things going on in Dickens's London or Mailer's New York, but when there is news about New Worlds, it is travel literature that becomes the crucial genre. If we want to know where it's at, we also want to know how to get there from here. Thus books like Castaneda's *The Teachings of Don Juan* and *A Separate Reality* are especially powerful because they take us from our present condition in civilization and then carry us all the way out.

Another excellent example of this contemporary revival of Renaissance travel literature is the story of transformation of Richard Alpert, Ph.D., into Baba Ram Dass contained in the Lama Foundation's "cookbook for a spiritual life." Called *Be Here Now,* the book begins where, in a sense, Tom Wolfe's *Electric Kool-Aid Acid Test* leaves off. In the closing scene of Wolfe's *roman verité,* Ken Kesey was caught in the predicament of a cultural movement that had broken away from its charismatic leader. Neither a political revolutionary nor a levitating guru, Kesey could do little but exhale the futility of "We blew it." That was in 1967, the peak of the hippie movement, and that is when Alpert broke out of hippiedom to begin his own journey to the East. Out of that journey he emerged as a classical yogi with all the Day-Glo washed off by the Ganges.

Perhaps *Be Here Now* is the best expression of how the Counterculture stands in the seventies; the flowers and bells along the Haight are gone, the millennial zeal has cooled, and in a mood of reflection and construction, the thirty-year-old hippies are consolidating themselves in a movement from cult to culture.

The sixties were a period of creative expansion; the seventies are a period of consolidation; but consolidation is no easy matter, for often the man who has the overwhelming experience is the one least able to routinize it. Moses saw the burning bush, but Aaron had to be the one to tell the people what it was all about. A clear expression of this dilemma is expressed in Carlos Castaneda's first book, *The Teachings of Don Juan.* Here we see the confident graduate student set out to write an anthropology dissertation on a Yaqui Indian sorcerer. Full of the certainties of American social science, Castaneda builds his scaffolding around Don Juan in an attempt to cage him within structural analysis and conceptual orders. Luckily for the reader, Castaneda is so perfectly divided a character that the social science scaffolding is kept for the introduction and appendix. What we see in between the scaffolding is the direct, powerful, and raw experience that overwhelms the graduate student and sends his scaffolding tumbling down. Understandably, Castaneda retreats in terror, for you cannot be a "man of knowledge" in two worlds, and Don Juan's knowledge was weakening Castaneda's grip on the solid realities of UCLA. Fortunately for Castaneda, UCLA didn't give him any choice, for academics know a threat to the paradigms of their normal science when they see it. And so Castaneda cannot return from the desert the same man who went in. But sorcery has its compensations, and the academic failure becomes a literary success.

In his second book, *A Separate Reality,* Castaneda gives up the phony social science of his first efforts and allows his own foolishness to lead him into a different kind of wisdom. With the scaffolding out of the way, Don Juan stands up in his own space. One cannot imagine an academic thesis-adviser who could fill the dimensions of Don Juan: wisdom, irony, whimsey, and playfulness, mixed with tragic strength, are all blended in the complete and yet dispassionate involvement of Don Juan in the development of his student. But if Don Juan towers over the professors, this sorcerer's apprentice is no Mickey Mouse. Clearly, Castaneda is a gifted writer who can handle the subtleties of narration and tone with the care of a

novelist; he can parody himself and mock his own ignorance
without ever tilting the balance away from Don Juan toward
himself.

Although Carlos Castaneda was not able to integrate the
separate reality of Don Juan with the reality of UCLA, most
of the other explorers in the occult are convinced of the
cultural necessity of just such an integration. And if one looks
at the occult from an historical point of view, he can see that
there is a relation between periods of imaginative growth in
science and periods of intense interest in the occult. Paracel-
sus and Copernicus in the sixteenth century and Dr. John Dee
and Francis Bacon in the seventeenth century are the two
sides of the coin of the scientific imagination. Newton himself
was a profound occultist, so one must recognize that the
imaginative innovators in science do not share the facile dis-
tinctions of their more bureaucratic followers. Perhaps the
best explanation of this process of discovery is in T. S. Kuhn's
The Structure of Scientific Revolutions. The textbooks of normal
science *contain* knowledge; but textbooks only tell specialists
what we already know, they do not make discoveries. Those
who do make the discoveries are working outside the containers in the dark of the unknown, and sometimes these discoveries literally occur in the dark, for the visions of the benzene
ring and the periodic table came in dreams.

For a good example of a dream landscape that is half
science fact and half science fiction, read the French book *The
Morning of the Magicians,* by Louis Pauwels and Jacques Bergier. From alchemy to the Zohar, from the lost civilizations of
earth to the influences of extraterrestrials, from crackpots and
hollow-earthers, everything you need to know about what is
out of sight and out of mind is here. But it is not the crazies
who are taken with this book; graduate students who wouldn't
be caught dead telling their thesis-advisers what they are
really into are deeply into the Pauwels and Bergier attempt to
reconstruct the secret, initiatic, and Pythagorean science that
is at once our past and our future. For all its fascination, the

book does not rest content with fascination alone, but insists that there remains a higher kind of sense to be made out of all the nonsense.

Because our culture is moving from one era to another, it seems like a radio that is caught in the spaces between two powerful stations; all kinds of noise and static are flooding in before we move on into the clear information and music of the next station. Demonology, Scientology, and an Alexandrian proliferation of cults overwhelm us along with the music of a coming age. One struggles to focus and lock in upon the proper wave length, but the attempt to separate the information from the noise becomes incredibly difficult. Too often one falls back on snobbery and prefers to see prophets who wear their loincloths discreetly under their doctoral robes. Castaneda, Alpert, Pauwels, and Bergier are much easier to take than the autodidactic scholarship of Erich von Däniken in his *Chariots of the Gods?*. Von Däniken's book says much the same thing as *Morning of the Magicians:* that there have been high civilizations in the distant past and that these civilizations were set up by the Sons of God mentioned in the Old Testament, that cataclysms destroyed these cultures, and that now all that remains is the enigmatic rubble in Easter Island, South America, and Mexico; but it is not what von Däniken says but how he says it that becomes so annoying. With all the virtues and vices of the self-elected savant, von Däniken raises his cranky voice and peers over his shoulder in search of a following.

A much more balanced and comfortable armchair approach to the inconceivable is in I. S. Shklovskii and Carl Sagan's *Intelligent Life in the Universe.* Here it becomes thinkable that when the Sumerians say that they did not build their cities but that the gods from the skies did, we should consider that they might be telling the truth. But if culture heroes from the stars shrink your sense of the importance of our planet and give you intellectual claustrophobia, then you should rediscover the strangeness of the inhabitants of earth by reading John

Lilly's *The Mind of the Dolphin: A Non-Human Intelligence.* Perhaps as interesting as the mind of the dolphin is the mind of John Lilly, M.D. The kind of man who works outside the paradigms of normal science, Lilly, like R. Buckminster Fuller, is one of those generalists who do not fit behind the frosted-glass divisions of a university department.

> I am a scientist. I try to be a kind of scientist called a generalist. This term "generalist" means that I do not any longer recognize the walls that have been arbitrarily set up between the sciences. The science of man is to me as important as the science of nuclear physics, or of biology, or of chemistry. In my opinion, the sciences are a continuum of knowledge broken only by the holes of the unknown. . . . For example, I need Christ's teachings, the works of Shakespeare, the writings of Aldous Huxley, Prokofieff's and Beethoven's concertos and symphonies, the paintings of Da Vinci, Le Tour Eiffel and the Empire State Building.[2]

Dr. Lilly is a walking one-man syllabus of Western Civilization, and it is his very miniaturization of his culture that enables him to surround it with spaces foreign to those who are locked within. Certainly the dolphin is the noblest savage of them all, and if Rousseau could be the paradox of a high-culture European who celebrated the virtues of savagery to put a finishing touch to the Enlightenment, then Dr. Lilly can be the paradox of a man who celebrates the very sciences against whose traditions he seems so bizarre. But paradoxes are appropriate, for what we learn from Dr. Lilly's dolphins is not zoology but anthropology. For a society strangling in its own technology, the dolphins express the ultimate in cultural design: no industrial class stratification, no polluting machines, no civilization with its repression-generated neurosis, but simply a medium through which the sensuous body moves beeping five-dimensional musical metamathematics to its companions and playing space-time chess with the stars. In this new literature of travel to other species, the Houyhnhnms of Dean Swift have been replaced by the dolphins of Dr. Lilly.

Whether we are traveling from the destruction of one universe to the creation of another or simply from one culture to another is not known. But what is known is that if one would create a universe, he must mix equal parts of Chaos and God; just such a mixture is to be found in all the new paperback testaments of the occult.

V

Introductions to Findhorn

No two places could be less alike than Findhorn and the Stanford Research Institute. SRI is one of the largest think-tank contractors for the Department of Defense and receives over sixty million dollars a year from government, industry, and foundations. Findhorn is a small spiritual community in the north of Scotland which is funded by faith that God will meet its needs if the community follows the esoteric "laws of manifestation." At SRI they talk to the important people of the world, but at Findhorn they talk to the plants in the garden. And the plants seem to like it so much that they respond by growing out of sand and blossoming in the snow. The miraculous garden of men and plants has become modestly famous, and in the last few years three different books have focused on the way of life there. It is time that the community of man and plants spoke for themselves, and thus *The Findhorn Garden* appears, written, photographed, and designed by the members of Findhorn.[1] But to appreciate the book within the context of contemporary global culture, one should read it alongside the Stanford Research Institute's recent monograph, *Changing Images of Man.*

Changing Images of Man is Policy Report 4 of SRI's Center for the Study of Social Policy. It is ironic to see a think tank calling for the creation of a new image of man in a new culture and then producing an American behavioral-science monograph that is part and parcel of the old world view. But it is even more amusing to realize that the people who would nod in affirmation at SRI's conclusions are the very ones who would be repelled by Findhorn. Nevertheless, the fact is that what is being talked about at SRI is being done at Findhorn.

Now questions of tremendous import arise. Could an image of humankind emerge that might shape the future, as the currently dominant images—man as the master of nature, inhabitant of a material world, and consumer of goods—our legacy of the past, have shaped our present culture? Could such a new image provide the bridge to carry us safely over to a postindustrial era? If so, what characteristics should the emergent image entail, such that it would be *both* feasible and adequate for the satisfactory resolution of the serious problems currently facing the society?

From the nature of contemporary societal problems, studies of plausible alternative futures, and our earlier considerations of the role played by a society's dominant image, we can postulate a provisional list of characteristics that a new image must possess if it is to become dominant and effective. At the minimum we believe it would need to: (1) provide a holistic sense of perspective on life, (2) entail an ecological ethic, (3) entail a self-realization ethic, (4) be multi-leveled, multi-faceted, and integrative, (5) lead to a balancing and coordinating of satisfactions along many dimensions, and (6) be experimental and open-ended.[2]

It all sounds well and good, but to those more familiar with the world of the behavioral sciences the monograph is really talking about the attempt of American social science (or what the report calls, with delusions of grandeur, "the policy sciences") to absorb culture into new forms of administrative control or cultural management. To do this effectively, Management must understand how culture works, how myths are generated, and how new images of man are created; therefore hitherto alien areas like religion and the humanities must be absorbed and pushed through the flow charts of systems theory. Although the report calls for a shift away from the image of man in which the individual is separate from nature, every line of the volume reveals the very mentality it is trying to escape. American social science, from the victory of the United States in 1945 to the victory of the North Vietnamese in 1975, tried to "develop" the world by replacing traditional cultures with behavioral-science ideologies of "modernization." The leaders of this movement were star-gazers in the courts of the imperial Presidents, savants like Walt Rostow and McGeorge Bundy. With the fall of Saigon and the failure of the Green Revolution, it is obvious that the historical limits to modernization have been reached; nevertheless, Policy Report 4 goes bravely on in the path of modernization as it struggles to replace the atavisms of religion and the humanities with "the policy sciences."

> Thus science [in parapsychological research] has legitimated systematic exploration of those realms of human experience in which our deepest value commitments have their source and which had hithertofore been left to religion and the humanities.[3]

To produce this report, the Center for the Study of Social Policy received a quarter of a million dollars from the Charles F. Kettering Foundation. They received the grant because the world of postindustrial society is an interlocking directorate of the corporate systems of government, foundations, universities, and industry. American social science is expensive, but any traditional historian could have told the social scientists and the foundation executives for a song that culture simply does not work the way "the policy sciences" think. New images of man do not spring from Policy Research Reports; all cultures begin in explosions of myth in the minds of prophets, mystics, visionary scientists, artists, and crazies. Whether it is in the dreams of Descartes, Alfred Russel Wallace, and Niels

Bohr, or in the visions of Buddha, Jesus, and Mohammed, culture springs from the depths no behavioral science can touch and still remain behavioral. The distance from prophecy to professorship is great, but even the founders of social science were much crazier than their contemporary routine followers, for Marx, Comte, Durkheim, Spencer, Saint-Simon, and Fourier were rather visionary in their sweep of ideas. It is, therefore, highly amusing to think that the administrators in the Kettering Foundation who granted SRI the quarter of a million would be horrified by *The Findhorn Garden* and could not see that the new world view and the new image of man are already embodied, not in a report, but in the living culture of the community of Findhorn.

Those who are likely to respond to *The Findhorn Garden* are those who can set it on the shelf alongside their copies of *The Book of the Hopi*, *The Tibetan Book of the Dead*, and *Journey to Ixtlan*. Now that we have taken in the visions of Hopi, Tibetan, and Yaqui cultures, it is time for us to welcome the stranger in our own Western tradition. From the esoteric point of view, of course, there is only one tradition. Whether we speak of kachinas, devas, djin, angels, or sprites, we are invoking a cosmology that is much the same around the world.

Industrialization tried to drive that cosmology out of men's minds, but now that the failure of the Green Revolution has dramatized the failure of the industrialization of agriculture, the underground traditions of animism can surface without any sense of embarrassment. It is the proponents of the agro-industry who need to be shamefaced now.[4] The iron winter of the industrial era is beginning its end. It is March all over the world, and now that a few crocuses are coming up through the snow, perhaps we can take heart to wait out the thirty-five years of coldness and death that remain before the New Age is in full blossom.

In this moment of late winter, we can see that preindustrial and postindustrial are coming together to put an end to industrial civilization. The landscape of the New Age is not a regressive, Crunchy Granola fantasy of nineteenth-century American agrarian life. We are not going back to what Marx called "the idiocy of rural life"; we are going back to nature with the consciousness of civilization behind us and the adventure of planetization in front of us. Urbanization and nationalism have reached their limits to growth along with industrialization, so the culture of the presently emerging future is one of decentralization of cities, miniaturization of technology, and planetization of nations. In the twenty-first century, the trees shall be great, the buildings small, and the miniature machines in just proportion to man. Animism and electronics are the landscape of the New Age, and animism and electronics are already the landscape of Findhorn.

The return of animism to the West comes just in time, for with the consciousness that comes of animism we can truly humanize our technology. We certainly cannot humanize technology with behavioral science, and no one argues against himself more persuasively than the technocrat.

> According to Simon Ramo, founder of TRW, a successful high-technology firm, technology is an instrument for predicting the future and solving social problems. Because man "must now plan on sharing the earth with machines," he must "alter the rules of society, so that we and they can be compatible."[5]

To manage men, you have to process them the way you do tomatoes: grow plastic varieties that can endure machine harvesting and pick them when they are green and unripe. The kind of men who can live compatibly with their machines are very much like the food they eat. Ramo is not talking about humanizing technology, he is talking about technologizing man.

Simon Ramo and others like him at TRW and SRI will try to alter the rules of society by using the policy sciences to program a new form of cultural management. Through an interlocking directorate of multinational corporations, labor unions, government, foundations, and universities, the Managers will point to the chaos they have created and appeal for special emergency powers to enable them to deal with the crisis through computer modeling and systems theory. And so industrial civilization, like winter in March, will die hard. But I don't believe that the problem-solvers can win out in the long run of cultural evolution, for all their dream-solutions become even greater nightmare problems. Problem-solvers, with their artificial intelligence and machine language, cannot tolerate ambiguity; they therefore cannot appreciate that organic forms generate life and culture, but that systems generate their linked opposite of chaos. Thus the next ten years are likely to be a world of systems and chaos, the world of the Manager and the unmanageable Terrorist. Enjoy the crocuses of Findhorn, but keep your overcoat on.

The people of Findhorn understand the place of technology in nature, and if they forget, the elves will soon let them know that the human parking lots are stepping on their toes. Modern man knows how to talk back to nature, but he doesn't know how to listen. Archaic man knew how to listen to wind and water, flower and tree, angel and elf. All the archaic cultures, Tibetan, Hopi, Sufi, and Celtic, are returning because they contain the very consciousness we need for the present and the future. The planetization of all the archaic cultures is coming at a time when it is desperately needed if we are going to evolve beyond the crisis of industrial civilization. Cultural evolution is not "being left to religion and the humanities," it is being led by religion and the humanities. And in evolution flexibility, risk-taking, and generalized adaptability count for more than bigness and strength. There is a weakness to bigness and power, and all the little cultures have returned to tell us that. The giant aerospace companies of Ramo's Los Angeles or Sony's Tokyo are in trouble. Once the great apes chased us out of the trees into the dangerous savannas, where, unable to swing happily where the great apes gibbered, we had to stoop down to pick up rocks. Now, the great apes are still back there in the trees. A new race of bullies in TRW and SRI and DOD are trying to push us around, and yet they are really pushing us out of materialism into the etheric dimension of a new adaptation.

And so the spiral of history turns; as we move away from industrial society, we come close to the animism of preindustrial cultures. Whether it is an American Indian at Oraibi, or a scholarly gentleman in a Georgian flat in Edinburgh, it is a vision that belongs to us, our future as well as our past. If we had taken our Shakespeare seriously, we might not have had to travel halfway round the world to discover the truth of Ariel's song:

> Where the bee sucks, there suck I:
> In a cowslip's bell I lie;
> There I couch when owls do cry.
> On the bat's back I do fly
> After summer merrily:
> Merrily, merrily shall I live now
> Under the blossom that hangs on the bough.

II

A generation ago Teilhard de Chardin made a prediction that has now become a cultural reality: "Like the meridians as they approach the poles, science, philosophy and religion are bound to converge as they draw nearer to the whole."[6] It was a fanciful thought that Père Teilhard had in those dark postwar days in Paris when *le néant* seemed to be the ultimate expression of Western civilization, but now it is exciting to hear the scientist and the mystic speak in similar terms. In his book *The Survival of the Wisest,* Dr. Jonas Salk put forth a theory of individual and group evolution that is remarkably similar to the work of David Spangler.

My aim here is to suggest that the tendency toward the separation and isolation of human groups according to EGO values that have formed and prevailed until now has prevented the recognition and expression of the BEING. They have favored the association of individuals according to EGO values rather than BEING values. If, as is suspected from what has been happening in the human realm, BEING standards are emerging with EGO values appropriate thereto, removing the encumbrance of essentially foreign EGO values which contributed to the development of enormous internal and external conflicts, then Man is entering upon a new phase of his evolutionary development.[7]

There are some playful ironies present in Dr. Salk's work, for, in many ways, he is dimly intuiting and vaguely expressing in his charts and graphs what is more clearly and substantially presented in Spangler's revelations. In a religious revelation, the concepts of evolution are expressed in emotional and spiritual imagery that enables all men to participate in a common mythology, but in a scientific expression of evolution there is always a pronounced elitist tone that gives one pause. David Spangler has addressed himself directly to this problem, and his transmissions are very clear on the point that we go astray if we begin to think of mankind in terms of the apocalyptically damned and the millennial elect. Nevertheless, Dr. Salk's description of the new evolutionary vanguard seems to fit Findhorn more than the American Academy of Arts and Sciences:

A new body of conscious individuals exists, expressing its desire for a better life for Man as a species and as individuals, eager to devote themselves to this end. Such groups, when they are able to coalesce through an understanding of their relatedness to one another and to the natural processes involved in "Nature's game" of survival and evolution, will find strength and courage in sensing themselves as part of the Cosmos and as being involved in a game that is in accord with Nature and not anti-natural. These groups will initiate movements which, in turn, will be manifest in their effects not only upon the species and the planet but upon individual lives. Their benefit is likely to be expressed in a greater frequency, or proportion, of individuals finding increasing satisfaction and fulfillment in life.[8]

In this vision of evolutionary change through well-being, Salk is coming very close to Spangler.

There is a simple difference between a person who is inwardly at peace and attuned to a source of strength and power greater than human level problems and one who is attuned to conflict with such problems and consequently to a consciousness of fear and anxiety and limitation. It is also known that people who are undergoing inner emotional stress are more accident prone, another consequence of this simple difference. Yet, it is just this simple difference that may be the key to the separation of the two worlds, not through something exotic, such as a miraculous translation of an elect few into some other plane, but through something as prosaic as people dying in significantly increasing numbers because they cannot live at peace within themselves and with their world nor can they create conditions of harmony. Earth itself, as a physical place, does not need to be cataclysmically altered in order to usher in the New Age.[9]

If the individual is to survive, he will have to have a life that does more than meet the basic need of his survival. It is one thing to stand with your fellow men in a subway in Tokyo or New York, and quite another to stand with them singing Handel's *Messiah*. Human evolution is not simply a matter of creating a technology for our survival, or, as many political scientists suggest, building a fresh ethic *for* our technology.[10] If we envision man as a clumsy beast who has to hurry to catch up with his own stainless-steel technology, then we fail to understand that technology and ethics spring from the very depths of culture, and in those depths, only the artist and the prophet can touch the very wellsprings of our being.

Culture does not spring forth from institutes financed by the state. Culture bursts forth from the unconscious: it rises from the cthonic powers of the earth and descends from the celestial visitations of the gods. Christian civilization flowed forth from a baptism in a river by a wild man of the desert; Islamic civilization sprang forth from a vision in a cave. You cannot create Christianity out of Newton's *Principia,* but you can create the *Principia* out of Christianity.

First things must come first, and all new cultures begin with the charismatic explosion of myth, of vision, of revelation. The new evolutionary culture that many scientists and scholars are calling for is not going to come from academic conferences, scholarly monographs, or scientific charts and graphs. The humanizing of technology is not going to come from liberal humanism; the ethics for the control of nature or genetic engineering is not going to be fashioned in committees. Planetary man is not going to solve the problems of postindustrial man, he is going to move out of the culture in which those problems and their solutions exist.

The seventeenth-century scientist did not learn how to solve the problems of the sixteenth-century alchemist; he learned how to stop looking for the salamander in the flames. Twenty-first-century man will not learn how to solve the problems of twentieth-century man: he will not learn how to control "the Green Revolution," he will learn how to talk and listen to plants; he will not learn how to control the weather, but to commune with devas of the wind; he will not learn how ethically to control the use of psychosurgery and electrical stimulation of the brain, but how to cure through etheric invocation. Planetary man will not learn how to humanize technology by thinking like a machine, he will humanize technology through animism. The new culture is the consummation of all previous cultures, for only the combined energy of our entire cultural history is equal to the new quantum leap of evolution. Animism *and* electronics are the new landscape of Findhorn: not the regressive infantilism of the drugged commune or the *Psychology Today* Disneyland of biofeedback, positive reinforcement, aversive therapy, psychosurgery, and ESB.

Culture is full of many surprises, because culture is full of the play of opposites. And so there will be scientists and mystics in the New Age. The Establishment tends to see the New Age as an era of full scientific realization, with the last atavistic remnants of religion found only in museums. The Counterculture tends to see the New Age as one of full psychic realization, with the last atavistic remnants of technology found only in museums.

To look at the American Counterculture today, one would guess from all the interest in Yoga, Zen, macrobiotics, and Sufism, that the East was about to engulf the West. But, as I have argued before, every vanishing cultural form has its most colorful expression at its sunset. In a Hegelian dialectic of *aufheben,* America is swallowing up and absorbing the traditional Eastern techniques of transformation, because only these are strong enough to humanize its technology. In the days before planetization, when civilization was split between East and West, there were basically two cultural directions. The Westerner went outward to level forests, conquer nations, and walk upon the moon; the Easterner went inward and away from the physical into the astral and causal planes. Now, in the case of David Spangler, and others like him at Findhorn, we can glimpse the beginnings of a new level of religious experience, neither Eastern nor Western, but planetary.

In an earlier age, the shaman fell into trance and lost his own consciousness as he was swamped by the unconscious. Later, the yogi learned to expand his consciousness through meditation and self-enhancing rather than self-immolating disciplines. Now prophetic figures like Spangler seem to be coming forth with a new form of consciousness: not an annihilation of sensory experience through yogic pratyahara, but an immediate dhyana or attunement so that the self becomes *figure* against the *ground* of being in God's consciousness. Here there is no mediumistic trance, no sitting in meditation for twenty years; one returns from the annihilation of all forms to the All annihilating itself into form. The religious discipline for this level of consciousness is not the sadhu alone in his cave, but the unique individual living in a universal community in which the group energies create the etheric embodiment of a god. With the fully individual self attuned to God and devas, the new man goes forth to act in a new culture in which action is not the negation of consciousness. Through Findhorn and the work of David Spangler, we can glimpse a science-fiction landscape of the future in which men and women move among the trees and machines, hearing the dryads in one and the molecular chorus of God in the crystal lattice of the other.

But let us not jump to conclusions and assume that the appearance of a new pattern means the contemptuous rejection of the old. *Aufheben* works through loving incorporation rather than hateful exclusion. The new spirituality does not reject the earlier patterns of the great universal religions. Priest and church, guru and chelas will not disappear; they will not be forced out of existence in the New Age, they will be absorbed into the existence of the New Age. Nowhere is this pattern more clear than at Findhorn, where yogis and Zen Buddhists, Jews and Protestant ministers sit side by side in the silent meditation of "Sanctuary."

David Spangler and Findhorn are, like Ficino and the Academy of Renaissance Florence, the seeds of a whole new cultural epoch. In *Revelation: The Birth of a New Age* we can see an entire world view; for many people this new world view will seem most alien. But cultural transformations do not proceed in easy transitions; they move in quantum leaps, and only a conversion experience or a revelation can give one the energy to leap across the abyss that separates one world view from another. A Roman Senator cannot become a Frankish Christian without first dying and being reborn.

In a way, it is unfortunate that those who will read David Spangler's book will already be converts to the new culture. The book is being printed by spiritual publishers in California and not intellectual publishers in New York; it will be reviewed and warmly received in the *East-West Journal* and not the *New York Review of Books,* but as Spangler's transmission has expressed it, we are already living in two worlds. Perhaps because I still travel back and forth between these two worlds, I would have more people consider Spangler's work. Of all the esoteric thinkers I know, he is the most lucid. He has none of the thaumaturgical obscurantism of the occultist, none of the syrupy sweetness of the blissed-out devotee, and none of the religious pride of the guru. To witness him in transmission is to take part in an overwhelming experience, and yet he is never overwhelmed or unbalanced. Always a sense of whimsey and playfulness returns to remind us that Revelation is not something supernatural and larger than life; it is what life is all about.

VI

Freedom, Evil, and Comedy

Let us begin with the most mysterious kind of laughter. Yeats, in "Lapis Lazuli," says that "Hamlet and Lear are gay;/Gaiety transfiguring all that dread." Why should a tragic hero laugh? Surely Yeats is not speaking about the moment of tragedy, but the moment just after. This is the comic moment: man steps out of his tragic action, observes his self and his former universe, and laughs. What Yeats is saying, then, is that Hamlet and Lear are free: free of evil, free of restraint, free of the body, and, of course, free of death. Free of death? As Rilke says: "Consider: the Hero continues, even his fall/was a pretext for further existence, an ultimate birth." Laughter then involves detachment, and detachment is a fundamental form of freedom. This freedom is the central value in comedy. But should we begin to speak about tragedy when comedy is our concern? Say that the opposite of freedom is evil; then both tragedy and comedy concern the problem of evil. Or put it this way: comedy offers a way out, a rebirth; tragedy also offers way out, but it is a way out *through* evil, through death. Comedy avoids evil; tragedy confronts it.

Greek tragedy is a tragedy of an evil predicament; the tragic error is not sin, not a conscious action of the self; it is a mistake of *being*. Individuation is the tragic error. Oedipus committed no sin; he was caught, caught in a world of circumstance, of contradiction, of limitation and pain: he existed as one in a world limited by the many. The only way out of this predicament is to cease being one in a world of many, to re-enter the world of the undifferentiated One. This is the ritual of rebirth in death, the ritual of the dying and resurrected god. Take Marsyas as an example of a tragic hero: did he challenge the god because he wanted to triumph over authority (a comic impulse), or did he challenge the god because he knew that the shudder of his discovered music would lead to his dismemberment, to his ecstasy? The latter. That is why Marsyas was not afraid to disfigure his cheeks to play his pipe. The goddess threw the pipe away, for what need has a goddess of music? She was a goddess and her body was no problem to her. Why should she trouble to make her cheeks ugly? It is only Marsyas, only man, who realized that the ugliness of the body, the disfigurement and the final dismemberment, could lead to an ultimate release.

Not so with Lear; he had to learn that. His is not a tragedy of predicament, but a tragedy of act. Lear's abdication is the horrible opposite of God's creation. God said, "Let there be light." Lear's abdication says, "Let there be chaos." Lear acts; therefore he must learn through action, through guilt and purgation. But Lear's guilt is not a guilt of being, an original sin of individuation; it is a sin of acting. Such action takes place only against a backdrop of belief, for who would act unless he first believed? That is why Lear's character interests us so much more than Oedipus's. Oedipus is any man who exists, but Lear is a man of personality and great energy, one whose energy ironically creates greater force in the divisions of his self. He is a man who wills, but a man who can find no image of his will in the world until he faces the image of his self on the heath. Lear's way out is not pagan, but Christian: guilt equals purgation, equals illumination and ecstasy. Now we see why the tragedy of our day has returned to a primitive tragedy of predicament. We no longer have that backdrop of belief, that hierarchical universe of Shakespeare. But our predicament is not one of individuation; it is a predicament of collectivization. The self is not defined in terms of eternity, God, or even, absolutely, in terms of itself. The self is defined by others. Each man looks over his shoulder at other men to find what he is himself. He is not responsible to himself; therefore he cannot know guilt, expiation, or tragic illumination. There is no meaning in all this, of course: we observe a line of men, each pointing the guilty finger at the man next to him. Here there is a regress to infinity, a disappearance of meaning in which no central term can be found by which the self can be finally known.

If tragedy is impossible because of the lack of a true and known self, comedy is all the more possible. The line of little men pointing the guilty finger at one another is comic. It is a mechanical piece of farce. If, then, tragedy cannot deliver modern man into freedom, we must look toward comedy. Genet knows this. In *The Balcony*, George sees the absurdity: there is no absolute self, there is only function, the function of a judge, a bishop, a general. If one acts, one commits oneself to a brothel of fantasies. Where is freedom? For the great man of action, that avatar of our age, the Chief of Police, freedom is in the immobility of becoming a statue. Only in absolute immobility can one avoid the contradictions and agonies of moving life. For Roger, who is rational and believes, the only way out is through castration. Castration in a brothel! The irony is obscene, but we must recognize it: Roger has severed his connection with life; he has denied his function. Functionless, he achieves the dubious freedom of annihilation. But for the common man the world continues; he will not accept its absurdity, but will continue to act through the convenient fiction that permits existence. It is our pious judge who says, "If every judgment were delivered seriously, each one would cost me my life. That's why I'm dead. I inhabit that region of exact freedom." So here we are: at the threshold of tragedy, we sense the possibilities of a comic existence. Laughter will permit us to endure the fiction, not with that platitude of ultimate belief, for we have seen that lead to Roger's dismemberment; no, we shall laugh at an absurd world to be free of it. Life begins to grow possible again. If Hamlet had laughed, he would not have worried about bridging the gulf between thought and action. Death had to teach him to be gay: that is his tragedy. In the middle of the battlefield the laughter of Krishna calls us to action, to freedom. The comedy awaits.

II

Comedy is a play about freedom, a play in which evil is mastered. It should not surprise us, then, that values will give us a means to distinguish kinds of comedy, much as we have above distinguished kinds of tragedy. Diffuse values are those in which the aims of life have not yet hardened into concepts; they are a tone that accompanies experience. The comic hero recognizes a restraint upon his freedom, but he is no reforming philosopher. The restraint here is a metaphysical one in the sense that evil is in the very nature of things, and the closest evil thing to the comic hero is his own impotent and limited body. What, then, should the comic hero do? Obviously, create a new and better universe. Impossible, of course, but if we assent to the fiction, we gain the possibility for laughter. We smile and think with buoyant heart, "If things were only so!" This kind of comedy does not embody a criticism of human folly; it embodies a celebration of imagination and human freedom. The new universe must be imagined as free of the evils of the old one. There should be no gods, old men should not have beautiful wives, but if they must, then they should have the virility of young men; beatings should not hurt and taxes should not be paid. Peisthetaerus in *The Birds* gains the impossible: he sets up his kingdom in competition with the gods, regains the virility of a young man, and wins the consort of the highest god. His wedding is the reconciliation of the opposites of man and god; the marriage celebrates the existence of a better universe; it celebrates the sexual joy of a new body. Here, of course, we are at the edge of farce, for farce is simply that which cannot be; that is, that which cannot be in the old scheme of things. But that is exactly what has been done away with. Farce is a grand way of saying, "To hell with everything!" To hell with learned men and their Latin, to hell with priests, to hell with old codgers who have pretty wives. This kind of comedy opposes sterility and age—those two horrors which really mean one thing: death. This kind of comedy has no lesson to teach; the nature of its suggested reform is patently impossible. Let Arlechino step out of his body and address it as the shadow it is. Let all the cuckoldry continue. The farce does not teach; it affirms and celebrates. We are freed from the nature of things to rejoice, even in immorality. In this comic universe, even immorality does not hurt. Rather say it is rascality. Who would want to censure Scapin or Ligurio? They show too much imagination and cleverness. The pompous old men in Molière's plays, with all their wisdom and wealth, have no life; they are rigid, they are not free. The rascality of Scapin or Ligurio is not evil; the very word "rascal" betrays our affection for them. Their evil does not destroy; it opens up new possibilities. With the abolishment of authority (all the gods, scholars, priests, and petty bureaucrats) a new freedom is achieved. This is, unfortunately, a primitive kind of celebration, one hopelessly impossible, but it is an imaginative kind of imitative magic that makes life easier to bear. It is like the Oaxacan rituals in which death is personified and mocked; it is like the Babylonian custom of the false king: the king for a day who is derided and then killed. The farce is always impossible, but this comic recognition of the impossible describes a universe that we desire.

III

As culture changes into civilization, a social order disengages itself from the moral order of the universe; ethics replaces metaphysics, and law replaces religion. No longer is evil seen merely in the nature of things; it is seen in the ways of men. Comedy of manners, comedy of types, satire, critical comedy: the proliferation of comic experience still recognizes an ethical rather than a metaphysical restraint upon man's freedom. "Civilization and its Discontents" replaces the anger at the gods. And what is civilization but a definite, articulate system of values? Here the comic playwright has a conscious lesson to teach. He does not affirm rascality and immorality; he affirms moderation and control, those two crucial values necessary for the survival of society. For with the repression that comes with society, there also comes a human need for an outlet, a need for bursts of license upon the stage. But as much as these bursts are enjoyed and permitted upon the stage, they are also criticized there. For this kind of comedy the basic activity is not the creation of a new universe, but the preservation of order from human folly. The conflict is not between freedom and restraint, but between license and moderation. This distinction between primitive and civilized comedies is, of course, not a temporal distinction; it is a distinction not between comic ages, but between modes of the comic imagination. *The Birds* seems to reach back in time to the primordial farce; it presents a comic mode that does not differ greatly from rituals of imitative magic. *Lysistrata,* however, is a comedy of the civilized mode; it presents a program for reform. The abolition of war seems ridiculous because it is so simple, but the ridiculousness does not lie in the nature of the proposed reform as much as it does in the nature of men that makes such reform impossible. Molière's *That Rascal Scapin* is also a primitive type; it recalls the simple *commedia del'arte* farce; but *The Miser* is a civilized comedy, a comedy of human nature and social folly. One is a play of folk imagination; the other is a play of conscious, artistic imagination. With plays of such articulate values, we see a parade of evil and human folly; we do not see an expulsion of evil from the universe. Such evil exists on stage because the playwright and the audience share a system of values which is critical of the presented variety of men. In *The*

Miser, we see the evil coming from human nature. Harpagon suffers from an obsession that destroys the balance of natural life; he is a threat to society; luckily his obsession makes him a danger to himself as well. Because of his fixation, he is easily controlled by flattery and money. But in this play it is not authority that is overthrown; it is authority that is invoked to save society from folly. Witness the *raisonneur* or the *deus ex machina* that often appears in these plays: Anselme in *The Miser*, the soldier of the King in *Tartuffe*, the Duke in *Measure for Measure*.

All plays which reveal articulate values do not find evil in human nature; some find it in society. In *As You Like It*, we see an almost Rousseauan idea of evil: evil exists in the world of society, the world of the court, because such a world corrupts human nature. In man's return to the forest of Arden, we see a return to simplicity, a return to a world in which Orlando does not have to take his food at the point of a sword. This strong sense of right and wrong enables the playwright to view experience rationally; it permits him to characterize evil as an obsession of passion or greed that destroys balance in the self and harmony in society—which takes freedom away from everyone. There is a moral center to this comic universe; sometimes it appears on stage, as in *Tartuffe*, sometimes it appears in the mind of the playwright or in the mind of the audience. In *The Alchemist*, we expect Lovewit to dismiss the evil and folly from his house and re-establish order; that he does not only heightens the moral awareness of the audience. The audience sees a parade of irrationality that continues to the end of the play.

Often in these plays, the complexity of the comic plot is itself a form of moral censure. The contrast between the simplicity of nature and reason and the complexity of human activity shows the hopeless folly of being human. *The Way of the World* is a highly intricate and stylized game of seduction and deception; the agonies to which these people go to avoid doing the obvious and natural thing, behaving rationally, is a strong source of comedy. It is as if we were watching the games of children, children who hate to work but go to Herculean labors in the name of play. In *The Way of the World,* civilized life has become a complex dance, and if one is to dance correctly, he must move with grace and intelligence. The clumsy, the low, the stupid: all these will stumble, and we, secure in our superiority, will laugh. Of course, we also laugh at the fops, at those fools who pursue elegance mechanically and stupidly and do not realize that sometimes life is clumsy and disordered. The ideal dancer turns the stumbling blocks of life into an occasion to display his own wit, brilliance, and flexibility. But lurking here in the midst of a rational universe, a universe that calls for intelligence to master it, is a subversive note. In Mirabell's smile is the recognition that, if the world is silly, good form must be maintained. And that, if nothing else, is civilization at its highest. But it would be a mistake to assume that high comedy is merely the comedy for an age of reason.

Shaw is a modern rationalist; however, the Shavian twist involves a change in what Bergson calls comic mechanization. In *The Miser,* it is the comic hero, Harpagon, who is mechanized, whereas society is flexible; in *Pygmalion,* society is mechanized, whereas Professor Higgins is flexible. For four acts Higgins seems the fool; then, by the Shavian twist, we are made into fools and Higgins emerges as the hero of enlightened common sense. Higgins is against conventionality, but not authority. Conventionality, for Shaw, is rational authority that has been corrupted by human folly into a mechanized and meaningless ritual. But despite this twist, Shaw's comic universe is as rational as Congreve's.

Brecht is another modern rationalist. His Marxism is the essence of rationalism, so that, in this sense, Brecht has the most articulate value system. In *The Good Woman of Setzuan,* the gods are comic because they are rigid; they persist in one direction although reality goes in another. Even when the gods collide with reality and receive black eyes, they do not learn but persist mechanically in their divinity. The gods are abstract; they are as useless as is religion to Marxist reform. Humans, however, are concrete. Because human nature is flexible and capable of change, the characters are not comic, but pathetic. We do not laugh at them (Brecht's alienation prevents that), we judge them. We judge them to be pathetic, or silly, or ignorant. Humans, when they affect to be divine, when they affect to be incapable of change, when they grow stiffly into religion, are silly and ignorant. Their humanity is moving in one direction, their alleged divinity in another; inevitably the two must collide. Shen Te and Shui Ta collide. There is no hope unless one steps out of the way: Shen Te, since her movements, like the gods', do not harmonize with fact. Fact collides with ideology. For the Marxist rationalist, the old ideology must move out of the way, so that the new fact may have room to create new values, and thereby free man from old, inadequate values.

For this rationalist Brecht, humans are comic because they want to be free in a stupid way. Mankind is like a mob that screams that the house is on fire and then blocks the exits. The playwright observes this from above; he sees that all can be saved if the mob will only file out in order. The playwright of freedom is, thus, the spokesman of control. Humans want freedom, but they ignorantly assert the self. They lust for power, but they do not see that in asserting their own power, they limit others, and thus have their own powers limited in return. Brecht calls for an ordered repression so that all may have the freedom that they desire. For collective man, salvation rests, not in the self, but in the State. This is religion "turned on its head": turn the other cheek, not because it is right in itself (for that is meaningless language), but because the classless utopia will be the result.

But another kind of comedy is lurking in this self-effacing society of collective man, and Frisch sees it. Biedermann is the archetype of the collective man, and Biedermann is simply stupid: he says one thing, and does another; he wants one thing, and achieves its opposite. Again we have another example of comic collision. In many ways, Biedermann is as traditional a comic hero as Harpagon. These comic heroes lack self-awareness; if they possessed it, they would no longer be comic, but tragic, for the collision of will and act is almost a tragic theme. However, Biedermann's stupidity saves him the anguish of a tortured conscience. It is only the articulate awareness of the audience and the playwright that recognizes the stupidity of the little man who can assume nothing on his own shoulders. We can laugh at him to free ourselves from the Biedermann within us. This is the moral. But the subtitle of *The Firebugs* is "A Morality without a Moral." Ultimately, there is no moral, for nothing can be proposed to take the place of all the Biedermanns. We cannot legislate human nature and its attendant folly out of existence. This awareness darkens the comedy. But this is only to say that comedies of articulate values do not celebrate, they criticize. We root out the evils of human nature and place them in caricature upon the stage to be free of them. We root out the bad elements of society to cleanse it, to improve it, and, of course, to enjoy the process. The comedy of moderation enables us to entertain on stage what we forbid ourselves at home. We gain the moral joy of censors who have the pleasure of reading the dirty books they are going to burn.

What we encounter, then, between diffuse and articulate comedies is the difference between primitive and civilized values (what the German sociologists might call the difference between the values of a *Gemeinschaft* and a *Gesellschaft*). High comedies have a lesson to teach: they show that the world is basically good and that evil is introduced into the world by human beings who lack moderation and control. These comedies affirm the wisdom of human authority as opposed to the barbaric folly of primitive, antisocial behavior. Farces and farcical comedies, on the other hand, affirm the vitality of human activity when it is free of restraint. Here the restraint is a metaphysical one, a restraint inherent in that small, but crucial piece of universe, the body, with all its threats of sterility, old age, impotence, and death. The farce is a strike for freedom, a strike against the gods. But the restraint upon civilized man is more complex: the enigmatic stars are hidden by cathedrals and battlements, and the force of restraint he most often feels is not the pressure of his own body, but the crowded buffetings in the street of bodies other than his own.

IV

Order, harmony, rational behavior, common sense: these are the values that other playwrights of our age cannot accept; they have been found to be the platitudes of a simpler but vanished past. Thought has turned in upon itself so that many modern comedies do not reveal values, they treat values. Since the modern playwright is skeptical about good, he must be skeptical about evil. The contemporary universe, as has been said often enough before, is a neutral universe. In contemporary comedies (that strange combination of the primitive and the civilized, of the tragic and the comic, of philosophy and ritual) the mode of restraint is epistemological. A large word, but one that simply means that man is imprisoned more by his mind than by his body or society. All of this means that man is a comic being when he believes that he can act with support for his beliefs. In Pirandello's *It Is So (If You Think So)*, Laudisi's laughter is not strange or inhuman; his laughter is based upon a very ordinary notion. The juxtaposition of a pie and a face is funny; for Laudisi the juxtaposition of man and truth is funny. For him nothing is more hysterical than man's affectation of knowledge. Fielding claimed that low characters who affect to be aristocrats are ridiculous and laughable; then, in Laudisi's terms, we must admit that human beings who pretend to a knowledge of truth are preposterously funny. What can man do in such a circumstance? He can think, and talk, and laugh; he can engage in no activity at all. Man waits for Godot, if there is a Godot, and in the meantime, he fidgets in the void. Vladimir and Estragon abuse one another to pass the time. Nietzsche's "Man would sooner have the void for a purpose than be void of purpose" comes immediately to mind. Vladimir and Estragon talk: they wonder if the tree is the same as it was yesterday, if it is Saturday or Sunday, if Godot will come. The mind questions uselessly. The absolute parody of reason is achieved in Lucky's speech. The modality of these plays is hardly celebrative, nor is it critical, for criticism means that something better is held in mind; the modality is analytical: everything is called into question, even the act of questioning itself.

If no belief is possible, then the world is absurd. The only difficulty in calling modern drama "the theatre of the absurd" is that there are several different kinds of absurdity. An absurd laugh dismisses the universe, but there can be several different reasons for this dismissal.

Laudisi's laughter is the nervous laughter of pain, the laughter that comes from a tortured consciousness. This laughter shades off into the tortured, hysterical laughter of near madness: the laughter of a great mind reduced to trivialities. Since belief in the great ideas is impossible, man forces his mind upon small things, fearing that if his consciousness is focused upon his predicament, he will go mad. This is the absurd laughter of the half-destroyed mind, the laughter of Pinter and Beckett. But there is a third laughter, a laughter that is the salvation of the mind and its pain; this is the human laughter of Ionesco.

Camus says that the absurd is lucid reason stating its limits; this means that we can laugh at reason because we know its limits. An absurd universe is a free universe. It is only when we believe in the mind that we are chained to events; once we lift our heads, grasp the absurdity of all theories, we are free, Consider Ionesco's pretty piece of metaphysics in *The Bald Soprano:*

MR. SMITH: As for myself, when I go to someone's house, I ring to enter. I think that everyone does the same, and that each time someone rings it is because someone is there.

MRS. SMITH: That's true in theory. But in reality things happen differently. You saw that just now.

Hope and expectation are the severest forms of bondage; they bind one to events. It is absurd to believe that for every effect there is a cause, but it is also absurd to believe that this statement will always be true. Occasionally there will be someone when the bell is rung. If one is committed to the absurd, he has no expectation, no hope; therefore he cannot be disappointed; he is absolutely free to take part in the fantasy of life. Those who cannot laugh at theories and systems are not free. In *Rhinoceros,* Berenger is the only one who achieves freedom; his co-workers cannot see the absurdity of their quotidian lives; they make the mistake of taking themselves too seriously, and thus are turned into beasts. Unlike Beckett's, Ionesco's laughter is really the laughter of great courage. For Beckett, the universe without the grand design is agony. But Ionesco is a humanist; he faces a world without meaning and asserts his humanity. He has the courage to be. In this he is close to his enemy, Brecht; but against the void, Brecht proposes a new system, a human system to take the place of the old Christian, divine one. Ionesco puts forth no system; he laughs at all systems and their futile vanity.

The fourth kind of absurd laughter expresses, not humanism, but mysticism. It is the laughter of Krishna, the laughter that regards the battlefield of human life from a suprahuman (or inhuman, if you will) point of view. Dürrenmatt's *The Visit* is a tragicomedy that investigates the horrible gulf that separates abstract goodness from concrete life. Taking his clue from Dostoevski's moral dilemma concerning the founding of a golden age at the cost of the murder of an infant, Dürrenmatt takes a difficult look at the irreconcilable natures of society and goodness. *The Visit* is a good answer to all facile schemes for social reform, for the villagers achieve freedom from poverty and disease at the cost of moral enslavement. In destroying Alfred Ill they have destroyed themselves, for the schoolmaster and the priest are compelled to disguise the murder as an act of justice. At the end of the play, the village that is supposed to embark upon a golden age has begun to rot. It takes little imagination to realize that wealth will mutilate the village as it has already mutilated Claire Zachanassian. The village no more has freedom than does Claire, whose millions have reduced her to an artificial stump of what was once humanity. In her suffering, Claire was human, but in the fanatical exercise of her will for revenge, she has hardened herself into wood. The poor man dreams that wealth brings freedom, but we see Claire's wealth turn nightmare.

> CLAIRE: . . . Your love died many years ago. But my love could not die. Neither could it live. It grew into an evil thing, like me, like the pallid mushrooms in this wood, and the blind, twisted features of the roots, all overgrown by my golden millions.

Sheer unchecked and unlimited exercise of the will does not bring freedom. The avenger is enslaved by his victim, the master by his slave.

But what of Alfred Ill? Is he free? *The Visit* is a tragicomedy because its heroine, Claire, is a comic figure, a grotesque one, but comic nonetheless; its hero, Ill, is a tragic figure: he confronts evil and his own fear and comes to terms with them in the face of death. He has his tragic vision, that is seen in his final scream: "My God!" What does Ill see? He sees that his death has not brought salvation for the village, that he is no scapegoat, that, in fact, his death has destroyed it. Ill, in death, passes out of the collective. He tells the Mayor that his death for him will be justice; "What it will be for you, I do not know." The villagers will have to come to terms with his murder by themselves, which they do not do. They huddle together and push off the blame by invoking the pathetic clichés of justice and morality. They do not understand the real terror of justice. They have not Ill's tragic vision. They cannot be redeemed by him. That is, perhaps, what Dürrenmatt means in the Postscript, when he says that "Ill's death would be meaningful only in the mythological kingdom of some ancient polis." In the community, not the collective. Ill gains freedom in death because death is the only private thing left for collective man. It is man's death that proves he is a self; it is his death that, paradoxically and tragically, gives his life meaning. Ill can now step out of the collective, look back, and laugh; he is free. That is the irony contained in the Cameraman's misinterpreting Ill's tragic "My God!" as a scream of joy. In many ways, it is; although only the audience, aware of the ironies, can be detached enough from the village to realize the comedy and the tragedy at once. This union of the tragic and the comic is the mysticism of the absurd. In *The Visit*, we watch Ill grow into this awareness.

But Pantagleize is this mystical absurd world view incarnate. He is not merely the simple innocent contrasted against a world of the depraved. Ghelderode's Pantagleize is no more a simple innocent than the fool in *Lear*. What mere simpleton would look on death and say:

> My poor friends, it wasn't worth dreaming such things and uttering such fine words. Here you are, done for. What was the good? I'm almost tempted to stay with you, to sleep your absurd sleep with you, lost in the equalitarian darkness. . . . We must part. . . . I shall never again bother myself with eclipses, or with my destiny.

Pantagleize, like all mystics, is free because he is not in "the fury and the mire of human veins." He will not share the equalitarian darkness with the executed revolutionaries, for that is the idea of death for the ordinary man. Pantagleize goes elsewhere; to end at the beginning, he steps out of his former universe, and laughs.

The absurd is, therefore, not merely lucid reason stating its limits: that is too polite, a mere apology of the mind for being inadequate to receive the universe properly. If comedy concerns the incongruous, the absurd concerns the incommensurate. The universe is incommensurate with the values of man. Man cannot relate his anxious endurance in time with the sheer horror of the universe's brute, physical endurance in time. All systems seek to overcome this; that is, they seek to relate man to the universe, body to soul. But the absurd is the denial of system, the ultimate metaphysic which teaches that relation is the cheapest form of identity. The comedy of the absurd demands a change of universes which is difficult to execute, because it is difficult to laugh at one's self; it is difficult to act when the myth that supports one's action is a recognized fiction. In this sense, modern art has the remorselessness of primitive religion. No man can easily will, like Marsyas, his own dismemberment. Yet the absurd drama inexorably shows that commitment to a rational, limited universe is the surest source of pain.

V

Comedy wants freedom; systems enable us to be free for something: ourselves, mankind, God. But in our deepest moments, we wish to be free of ourselves, mankind, and God. Thanatos? Perhaps, but the ultimate in comedy is not death and tragedy. The ultimate in human comedy is to become God, a definitionless God. What we wish for in comedy is to usurp from God the right to the last laugh.

The farce, the comedy, the absurd drama: what we are really talking about with all these genres is simply the anthropology of values: the difference in values of a folk community, a city-state, and an industrial nation-state, a collective. The hero of the farce demands that the universe be changed; the hero of the comedy demands that society accommodate itself to his will; the absurd hero makes no demands: the universe is beyond mere belief and society is incorrigibly a hoax. The absurd hero withdraws into himself, or rather he makes a gesture of his self: the infinite expressions of the human face gain the exact freedom of an immovable, absurd mask. Half the audience will see the mask as tragic; half the audience will see the mask as comic. The audience will be right, for the human condition does not change; we have the same ancient choice: we can laugh or we can cry.

VII

The Ends of Art

Not so very long ago, literary culture was the dominant paradigm for intellectual society as a whole. There were giants in those days, and the shadows cast by an Eliot or a Faulkner extended over oceans and continents. Then something happened, or, rather, something no longer continued to happen. Books were still published and read, some forty thousand a year in all, but they were more information than art. In a world of new technology and new life styles, social science seemed a more appropriate vehicle for turning data into ideas. With *Psychology Today* pulling in one direction, and *Rolling Stone* in the other, the literary quarterly cracked up, and *Partisan, Hudson,* and *Sewanee* became so many potsherds left about for archaeologists to decipher.

The industrial world had always been hard to take for writers, but there had been something heroic about their willingness to fight with it. In the genius of a Yeats or a Lawrence there was a certain perverse flying in the face of facts, and an obstinate insistence that great art could more than handle the industrial hordes of the Philistines. No doubt, the artist felt that a well-aimed word was missile enough to bring Goliath down, but in postindustrial society the enemy was no such obvious target. The factory changed from a dark Satanic mill to a Bell & Howell Human Development Corporation where systems managers engaged in sensitivity training. The enemy was no longer a savage brute to be contrasted with the shepherd-poet; he was a social scientist fighting to win minds through words in countless articles, reports, monographs, books, and even best-sellers. Never mind that his prose was ugly. A generation raised on television no longer knew what prose style was: give them pictures and collages, a few questionnaires thrown in for calligraphic contrast, and who could tell that the prose was gone?

How can an artist fight with banality? The keen edge of the sword is designed to encounter a resisting medium, but how can one slice through *shlock?* The artist is bred for heroic encounter; what immolation is possible except self-immolation? And so the reincarnation of D. H. Lawrence became Yukio Mishima.

Suicide seems to be the fate of many artists these days: Sylvia Plath, John Berryman, and Anne Sexton. Those who linger on do not seem to do so in good health; some, like J. D. Salinger, lapse into a catatonic silence; others, like Saul Bellow, become voices of resentment and complaint.[1] At least, no one is kidding himself any more; the age of The Artist is over, and the posturing of the avant-garde is as ridiculous as Moral Rearmament.

The avant-garde is dead and with it Pound's dictum "Make it New." Civilization has run out of material, and so everything is in revival: the revival of the twenties with *Gatsby,* the revival of the thirties with Cole Porter, of the forties with *The Summer of '42,* of the fifties with *The Last Picture Show,* of the sixties with *American Graffiti.* Since it is hard to revive the seventies before they are over, film-makers have sensed our apocalyptic mood by producing a gaggle of disaster epics.

All is in revival because art is dead, and art is dead because we tried to make an entire culture out of art and The Artist. But art grows out of culture and is fed by culture. If art has to feed upon itself for mythology, it will die; like a stomach with nothing in it, it will soon digest itself. How can we have art now that all traditional cultures, industrial and preindustrial, are dying? In these declining years of the second millennium A.D., what is left to us but apocalypse?

In a society in which one is swamped with forty thousand books and one million scientific papers a year, the environment is not really nature, but information. We move, as Baudelaire said, through a forest of symbols. It becomes necessary, then, for some fool (no expert would dare) to take all that information and tranceform it into significant modes of consciousness. Since novel and slim volume of verse do not threaten our view of reality, one has to play around with reality itself in nonfiction. If our culture is threadbare, we need to turn it inside out before we can darn it. But to turn reality inside out, one has to move into mysticism. For the threadbare intellectuals of London, Paris, and New York, this mysticism is an unsettling inversion of their whole Marxist-Freudian world view.

It is a rich irony that the world of social science should produce the mystical works of Carlos Castaneda, but there are historical precedents, for the Papacy produced the works of Michelangelo. In expressing the tension between individualistic secular liberation and ecclesiastical mythic forms, Michelangelo stood in the doorway between two worlds. And so do we now. Castaneda may not fill Michelangelo's shoes, but in our contemporary planetary renaissance, he stands in a similar position. In bringing together the prehistoric landscape of archaic Mexico and the posthistoric landscape of Los Angeles, this nonfiction writer has shown us that the Yaqui shaman and the UCLA anthropologist are both members of vanishing cultures.

The works of Castaneda do for us now what novels used to do, and the short essays of Dr. Lewis Thomas do for us what poems used to do. In fact, *The Lives of a Cell* is a slim volume of verse, a collection of the genre "poems of description and meditation." The kinds of thoughts we used to take in the form of lyrics on nature and mortality are here in "Antaeus in Manhattan" or "Ceti." But it is not only the fact that nonfiction is raised to the level of art that brings the work of Dr. Castaneda and Dr. Thomas together; it is the fact that both of these informational fools have had to resort to mysticism to make sense of the universe.

The mystical theme that runs throughout *The Lives of a Cell* is that our individual minds are cells in some larger super-organism. This is a conclusion that many different contemporary writers seem to reach, whatever different paths they may take: Chardin on the path of theology, Soleri in architecture, Clarke in science fiction, and McLuhan in communications. To see the thought come up in scientific guise in the work of the president of the Memorial Sloan-Kettering Cancer Center should give the behaviorists something to think about.

> We pass thoughts around, from mind to mind, so compulsively and with such speed that the brains of mankind often appear, functionally, to be undergoing fusion.
>
> This is, when you think about it, really amazing. The whole dear notion of one's own Self—marvelous old free-willed, free-enterprising, autonomous, independent, isolated island of a Self—is a myth.
>
> We do not yet have a science strong enough to displace the myth. If you could label, by some equivalent of radioactive isotopes, all the bits of human thought that are constantly adrift, like plankton, all around us, it might be possible to discern some sort of systematic order in the process, but, as it is, it seems almost certainly random. There has to be something wrong with this view. It is hard to see how we could be in possession of an organ so complex and intricate and, as it occasionally reveals itself, so powerful, and be using it on such a scale just for the production of a kind of background noise. Somewhere, obscured by the snatches of conversation, pages of old letters, bits of books and magazines, memories of old movies, and the disorder of radio and television, there ought to be more intelligible signals.
>
> Or perhaps we are only at the beginning of learning to use the system, with almost all our evolution as a species still ahead of us. . . .

The mechanism is there, and there is no doubt that it is already capable of functioning, even though the total yield thus far seems to consist largely of bits. . . . There may be some laws about this kind of communication, mandating a critical density and mass before it can function with efficiency. Only in this century have we been brought close enough to each other, in great numbers, to begin the fusion around the earth, and from now on the process may move rapidly.[2]

What is making the process move more rapidly is not just global television, but global mysticism. Individuals less centered in their egos are discovering the patterns of convergence and synchronicity in their lives and the life of the new culture. It almost seems as if the consciousness of a racial, planetary Being were surrounding civilization, compressing it, and turning it into a miniaturized artifact of the past. The artist caught inside civilization feels the pressure and is demoralized because he is holding on tight to his civilizational identity; witness the mythologizing of the ego in the work of Norman Mailer. It is the work of the artist to reinterpret the world, but since the civilized artist cannot understand this new world, he has chosen to perish with the old.

With the death of the art of civilization, the art of planetization is born. Once the romantic artist, like Yeats, made the emerging nation, like Ireland, conscious of its national identity; now the planetary artists are trying to make the races conscious of their emerging planetary identity. The old artist sculpted with stone, painted on canvas, or told stories about a day in the life, but whether it is conceptual art, nonfiction, or the music of Stockhausen, the new medium is information itself. The place where information is densest is the university; and that is why many of the new artists have come out of that setting, not as artists in residence or professors of creative writing, for those are civilized roles, but as jugglers of information. Where the expert is enthroned, there the fool is forced to say "uncle," but masks his subversion by crying "nuncle."

To understand contemporary culture, you have to be willing to move beyond intellectual definitions and academic disciplines. You have to be willing to throw your net out widely and be willing to take in science, politics, and art, *and* science fiction, the occult, and pornography. To catch a sense of the whole in pattern recognition, you have to leap across the synapse and follow the rapid movement of informational bits. You treat in a paragraph what you know could take up a whole academic monograph, but jugglers are too restless for that: the object of the game is to grasp the object quickly, and then give it up in a flash to the brighter air.

VIII

Evil and World Order

How is it that when we try to do good we can often end up
by creating greater evil? The Declaration of the Rights of Man
in 1789 ended in the Reign of Terror and the rise of the
dictatorship of Napoleon. The temporary dictatorship of the
proletariat in Russia ended up in the permanent dictatorship
of the ex-proletariat in the new bourgeoisie of the Communist
Party. America fought a revolutionary war against the British
Empire, and then became an empire fighting to suppress a
guerrilla war of national liberation in Vietnam. But these *enantiodromias* are not restricted to the contradictory world of
revolution and politics, for the Green Revolution started out
as a project to feed the masses of starving India, and then
ended up as an Americanization of Indian agriculture in
which the rich got richer and the poor got poorer through the
introduction of the petrochemicals, fertilizers, tractors, and
large land holdings of the modern agro-industry. The industrialization of the planet and the global distribution of medi-
cal services have increased the population so that now more
people are suffering than ever before. This year four hundred
million people are dying of starvation.

Liberals like to speak of progress, especially of progress in
terms of "modernization," but hunters and gatherers have
more leisure time than we have and no way of institutionaliz-
ing conflict in warfare. Every step toward progress, whether
it is the agricultural revolution of 9000 B.C., the urban revolution of 3500 B.C., or the industrial revolution of 1770, has

carried with it an equal and opposite horror. As Homer recognized long ago, your unique excellence is also your tragic flaw; your greatness hobbles you. We have tried to do good in modernizing the planet through industrialization, but the internal contradictions of industrial society are beginning to become painfully visible; now some ecologists are predicting that the population of the earth will drop a hundredfold in the next ten to twenty years.[1] If this is the case, then the entire Industrial Revolution and the whole philosophy of progress which went along with it will culminate, either through famine, ecological catastrophe, and economic disorder, or through thermonuclear war, in the greatest cataclysm in the history of the human species. When this happens, it will not be because people were consciously trying to do evil; in many cases, the leaders were trying to do good.

If evil can grow out of our efforts to do good, it also seems to be the case that good can grow out of our efforts to do evil. The Roman military engineers built the roads that the Christian missionaries traveled to convert an empire. The British executed by firing squad the Irish rebels of 1916, and thus helped to free Ireland. The Nazis executed the six million, and thus helped to bring the state of Israel into existence. But much of this seems unconscious, for those who do evil certainly do not plan to have good result from it, and those who think they are working for progress do not wish to create apocalypse. The inventor of the aerosol spray did not wish to destroy the ozone layer of the planet, but whether it is dynamite, atomic energy, psychosurgery, or genetic engineering, it does seem to be the case that our very unconsciousness of these *enantiodromias* increases the likelihood of evil emerging from our acts. It is no longer safe to assume that good intentions are enough. One can wreak havoc with benevolence as well as with malevolence; therefore we have to stop and call into question the ideas of progress and philanthropy upon which modern liberalism is based.

A new race of liberals is arising to seek "The Creation of a Just World Order,"[2] but if we remain as unconscious in this second global wave of liberalism as we were in the first wave which came at the end of the Second World War, then we are likely to create untold horror on a planetary scale. If the Green Revolution can increase starvation, if antibiotics can be described as a threat to the evolutionary viability of the human species, if the entire edifice of modernization can be seen to be a curse, then how can we assume that those who write proposals for a "Systems Approach to World Order"[3] know what they are doing? If a thing as tiny as an aerosol spray can generate intense scientific debate about the future of life on this planet, then what of a grand scheme of a handful of academics for creating an entire world order?

We are like flies crawling across the ceiling of the Sistine Chapel: we cannot see what angels and gods lie underneath the threshold of our perceptions. We do not live in reality; we live in our paradigms, our habituated perceptions, our illusions; the illusions we share through culture we call reality, but the true historical reality of our condition is invisible to us. How can you fix up history if you cannot see it? And what if history cannot be fixed from inside history? What if the attempt to fix human history is an effort to seek out the dark with a searchlight?

> The optimum long-term scenario foresees a world order where human needs are adequately satisfied. The greatest number of persons find the highest levels of satisfaction, thanks to the equitable distribution of resources that represent the necessary, if not sufficient, conditions for fulfillment of the hierarchy of human needs. Such a distribution is achieved with the minimum of coercion and the highest humanly attainable degree of voluntary cooperation between individuals and groups. This, truly, is the route to paradise on earth.[4]

We like to think that Truth or the Good is knowable, isolatable, and implementable. There is the Truth; it is either capitalism, or Communism, or General Systems Theory. We implement the Truth, and the Good follows. Surely, if history were that simple, we would have fixed it up a long time ago. After all, we have been genetically human for some forty thousand years. We have not solved the riddle of humanity because we are still thinking we can discover the truth and express it in an ideology. The Truth can never be an ideology; Truth is that which overlights the conflict of opposed ideologies.[5] Opposites are polarities that create a field. The sky is not a place, it is a relationship between earth and sun. You cannot isolate its blueness in a bell jar and distribute it to the masses for the good of mankind. The sky is empty, and yet it is a form, a form of relationship. In the wisdom of the Buddhist sutras, we would say that "Form is not different from Emptiness, Emptiness is not different from Form."

Because the Truth is not an ideology, it is best embodied in paradoxes and koans, for paradoxes are relationships of opposites. What is the dark but the medium of light?

Consider the following paradox. To commit evil effectively, either in the Mafia or the National Socialist Party, one must accept authority and tell the truth *within* the group. It is the old case of honor among thieves. Thus to commit evil effectively, one must do some good. If every Nazi had lied to every other Nazi, the party and the government would have dissolved into entropy. Therefore, in order to exist, things need integrity, literally. We may call this literal integrity, the moral order, or, better, the Tao. It would be simple if we could identify existence as the Good, and entropy as the Bad, but dissolution is involved in the life of forms. For example, life on earth evolved because it was seeded with the atomic material in space left over from dead, exploded stars. General Systems liberals, who lack the Homeric tragic vision, like to talk about the systemic invariance of form as described in the revised thermodynamic equations of Prigogine,[6] but systems only violate the Second Law for a time, and in the stream of time, the thermodynamic irreversibility of events still continues. Even stars die, and they must die if their material is to be made available for the evolution of life on other planets. The

Tao composts stars the way we compost garbage. Thus the drift of forms toward entropy is the generation of a creative disequilibrium vital for change, transformation, and evolution. A static form of life which is systemically invariant is, from another point of view, energy which is unavailable for work. Life requires death if it is to be released from the prison of its form. Again, "Form is not different from Emptiness, Emptiness is not different from Form."

Let us paraphrase Kant's old argument from the *Critique* to say that we can conceive of objects without existence: unicorns; but we cannot conceive of existence without objects, without something existing. And so it is with goodness: we can conceive of persons without evil: saints and avatars; but we cannot conceive of persons without goodness, for even Hitler required some goodness to maintain the integrity of his own existence. Thus the Good, the moral order, the Tao, becomes even more basic than the Bad. Perhaps now we can see why Mephistopheles felt that his work was so frustrating:

FAUST: Who then are you?
MEPHISTOPHELES: Part of a power that would
  Alone work evil, but engenders good.

Consider another paradox. When individuals try to do evil, they often appeal to the Good as their *raison d'être*. Even in the act of perpetrating horrors, people appeal to noble ideals, and by invoking them, validate them. Neither the Nazis nor the Ku Klux Klan say: "Follow us because we're evil and abominable."

But what of Satan worshipers, Hell's Angels, or the followers of Charlie Manson? To understand the worshipers of Satan, we had better start at the top and work our way down. Let us return to Faust's conversation with Mephistopheles:

FAUST: What hidden meaning in this riddle lies?
MEPHISTOPHELES: The spirit I, that endlessly denies.
  And rightly, too; for all that comes to birth

Is fit for overthrow, as nothing worth;
Wherefore the world were better sterilized;
Thus all that's here as Evil recognized
Is gain to me, and downfall, ruin, sin,
The very element I prosper in.[7]

The Satanic principle is the abhorrence of existence. It is a hatred of everything that is other than the rich darkness of the void. For Satan, God is intent on a cosmic ego trip in which all works out to His Higher Plan. Satan is the spirit who denies the plan, who pushes every napalmed baby in God's face and says: "See this! You wanted to create a universe; well, look at what is in it. But, of course, this is only a small thing that works out to unimaginable Good in your Higher Plan." The horror of existence is so extreme for the Satanist that he must strive to pervert all forms. In raising the horrible to our eyesight, he tries to show us the hidden horror that is, for him, the true nature of existence. And so the followers of Satan will revel in perversity because it is the negation of all that we value: the disciples of Charlie Manson will jab the knife and fork into the stomach of the pregnant Sharon Tate, the Hell's Angels will make sacraments out of urine and excrement, and the Nazis will make tobacco pouches out of the breasts of young women.

Yet this Satanic evil which tries so hard to be cosmic has, as Goethe realized, a certain petulance to it. The Devil seems like a child acting up in a desperate longing for punishment, or like a child who has not been invited to a birthday party and so conspires to ruin the whole show. In the very act of spoiling the party, he shows how important it is to him. Willful conscious evil, therefore, seems to reflect an affirmation of the Good. To work to frustrate God is to work *for* God; it is to have one's whole identity dependent on God's next step in the Higher Plan.

One can see why the Gnostics preferred to speak of the right and the left hands of God and to see Christ and Lucifer as the two sides of the Demiurgos who creates the physical universe. Lucifer creates the Fall into matter; Christ redeems the Fall by taking the soul up into spiritualized matter in his Mystical Body and thus makes of the entire manifest universe a work that transcends the opposites of void and existence. "Form is not different from Emptiness, Emptiness is not different from Form."

It is easy to see that the extremist, the Satan worshiper, is a person of twisted religious sensibility, but what of the apathetic soul, the person who is totally uninterested in matters of good and evil? Well, if he is totally uninterested, he will be no problem to anyone; he removes himself from the game of existence entirely. If he remains interacting at *any* level, then he is merely a liar and proves by his actions his interest in continuing the game of existence.

So when we come down to it, the most perplexing form of evil, and especially so for all idealists, is that kind of evil which comes out of our efforts to do good. Why does liberation lead to tyranny, medicine to suffering, and the Green Revolution to famine? Liberalism makes an easy whipping boy, for it is clear that LBJ's War on Poverty did little good, but do all forms of doing good create evil? When a mother nurses her crying baby, is she doing evil? Evil may come of it if the baby grows up to be Genghis Khan or Hitler, but the cause of that evil is not the mothering act.

What, then, is the difference between a mother nursing her baby and a president declaring war on poverty? Jesus said: "By their fruits ye shall know them." If the fruits of an action are bitter, should we not begin to suspect that the seed was bad? Perhaps when we try to do good without love, we create evil. Perhaps when we try to do good without love, we are not really doing good, but simply running for re-election, puffing up our self-image as a noble being, or trying to gain power over a situation by controlling it through charity and philanthropy.

Take the famine. Four hundred million people are dying

this year. If we do not feed them, people will die; if we do feed them, more people will die. We are in a double-bind; ultimately, we will feed them because it makes *us* feel better to do something. Our desire to do something about it is a way of avoiding the feeling of impotence before death. But has not our attempt to turn from death created this even larger form of death which now confronts us? How large must this horror get before we turn to stare it full in the face? Will it take a thermonuclear war, that exquisitely rational form of Terror?

The liberal often has a horror of death, as if it were not part of life, but the ultimate affront to man's control and rational management. Death is accepted in a society of hunters and gatherers, but in our progressive society, we turn from it and recreate it everywhere around us on a scale that staggers the imagination. Look into the eyes of a liberal talking about the famine and you will see that he cannot help but believe that life is a problem to be solved, that if we send in the Peace Corps, Care Packages, or the Marines, then the problem will be solved, life will become manageable, and evil will be under control. This kind of liberal labors, as Faulkner would say, "in a fury of abhorrence." He wants to feel power, power to change the course of rivers with dams, to grow wheat out of sand, to conquer cancer, and to walk on the moon. He is centered in his ego, and when his power over an environment is frustrated, when his solutions turn into even greater problems than the problem they were intended to solve, he lashes out in impotent rage and his unbalanced idealism flips into its linked opposite.

There can be no love in one who does not love himself, and one can only love himself if he has the compassion that grows out of the terrifying confrontation with one's own self. To look into one's own shadow is to learn compassion for the shadow of others, and if one has no compassion for himself, then he can have no compassion for others. If you hate yourself with a fierce loathing, you may try to run from your own shadow in a campaign to do good, not for love, but to rescue your ego and convince yourself that you are not evil. In the eyes of how many world-transforming activists do we see dissonance, anxiety, fear, and self-loathing? They would reform the world, but they cannot even reform themselves, much less quit smoking. They are running from evil, the evil they have not confronted in terror inside themselves, and thus their unbalanced idealism is inflicting the Terror upon all of us. In the Irish Revolution, the revolutionaries claimed that there was no evil in Ireland, that the English brought it in with their conquest, and that if the English were driven out, evil would be driven out with them. But the country that dismissed evil from its consciousness of itself was overwhelmed with evil.[8] Sixty years after the rebellion, the murder still goes on.

Idealistic reformers are dangerous because their idealism has no roots in love, but is simply a hysterical and unbalanced rage for order amid their own chaos. Lacking the tragic sense of life and the capacity to endure, they break down with a few frustrations of their efforts to do good and be loved, and flip into their opposite. The artist *manqué* became the SS officer.[9] And so I fear all these General Systems Theorists and computer scientists who would manage the planet. The warning that Jung sounded needs to be remembered:

> Today humanity, as never before, is split into two apparently irreconcilable halves. The psychological rule says that when an inner situation is not made conscious, it happens outside as fate. That is to say, when the individual remains undivided and does not become conscious of his inner opposite, the world must perforce act out the conflict and be torn into opposing halves.[10]

The first stage of illumination in Tantric Yoga comes when the awakened shakti, the psychic energy, makes one's darkness visible. The shakti of Mother Nature is now making the darkness of the human race very visible. We may, thus, take heart that we are beginning to experience illumination. We are experiencing the initiation of the human race into a new level of consciousness, and that is a very terrifying experience. It does no good to turn and run from the terror of our darkness into light; we must sit it out: zazen. We must take our counsel from *The Tibetan Book of the Dead* and realize that these frightening projections of famines, economic disasters, ecological catastrophes, floods, earthquakes, and wars are all only the malevolent aspects of beneficent deities. If we sit and observe them, do not identify with them, but remember our Buddha-nature, we will not be dragged down by them into an incarnation of the hell they prefigure.[11] If we run from them, we validate them; we give the projections the very psychic energy they need to overtake us. Then, as Jung has pointed out, the situation will happen outside as fate.

So I think a "Strategy for the Future" is not in Lazlo's General Systems Theory, but in *The Tibetan Book of the Dead*. To grow conscious of one's shadow is to develop a capacity to endure and prevail. Traditionally, the humanities had the strength and tough-mindedness of the tragic sense of life. The visions of a Faulkner, an Eliot, or a Yeats made the positivism of the social sciences seem a bit shallow. With the modernization of the university, the humanities, much like the Third World in general, have been subjected to an enforced transformation into social science. One looks in vain for heart's wisdom and passionate intellect in the academic world of the humanities; Lazlo speaks more than his volume for what philosophy has become in the modern world.

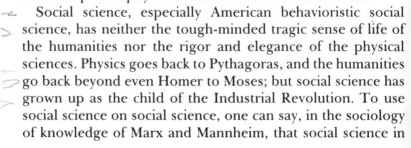

Social science, especially American behavioristic social science, has neither the tough-minded tragic sense of life of the humanities nor the rigor and elegance of the physical sciences. Physics goes back to Pythagoras, and the humanities go back beyond even Homer to Moses; but social science has grown up as the child of the Industrial Revolution. To use social science on social science, one can say, in the sociology of knowledge of Marx and Mannheim, that social science in

general, but General Systems Theory in particular, is simply
the ideological camouflage for the emergence of an industrial, managerial elite. In the early stages of industrial society,
sociology was a challenge, a slap in the face of the old, aristo-
cratic landowning elite of traditional civilization; in advanced
industrial society, social science has become the ideology of
the managers who joined corporation, government, think
tank, and university together in the interlocking corporate
systems of the postwar world.

> Last, but not least, we understand that greater diversity
> at higher levels goes hand in hand with smaller populations
> at these levels. There are fewer cells than molecules, fewer
> organisms than cells, and fewer societies than organisms.
> Ultimately there is but one global ecosystem, which, to-
> gether with its human components, forms the world system
> which is the principal object of this inquiry.[12]

There is but one ecosystem, and, by implication, there can
be but one General Systems elite to understand it and manage
it.

Under its founder, Ludwig von Bertalanffy, General System
Theory started out as a protest against mechanism in favor of
organism;[13] in this development of a philosophy of organism,
von Bertalanffy was coeval with Whitehead. The roots of systems theory were embedded in the traditions of European
philosophy and science, but in the events of the Second
World War these traditions were surrounded by the routines
of the American bureaucratization of science and technology.
With the development of cybernetics, information theory,
and with the development of management routines for complex projects like the atom bomb and the exploration of
space, the philosophical approach of von Bertalanffy was
streamlined into the systems science of the think tanks of the
Department of Defense. The organism simply became a more
intricate machine of "complex feedback loops," and in the

development of artificial intelligence at MIT, Professor Marvin Minsky could exclaim: "What is the brain but a computer made out of meat?"

The organic function simply became one input among others. Thus the philosophy which began as an attempt to avoid reductionism created a new notation for reducing the organism to a new form of mechanism. The ultimate extension of this new systems form of reductionism was to create the computer model for the life of the planet in the work of Forrester, Meadows, and Mesarovic. And so yet another *enantiodromia* proved that what starts out as one thing can end up as its exact opposite. If this can happen with the founder of General System Theory, what is to stop it happening to its follower, Ervin Lazlo?

The General Systems approach to world order might start out as an effort to manage the planet for the good of mankind, but as the American and Soviet engineers came together, the philosophical traditions of the two countries would be politely avoided in an agreement to speak the common language of systems notation. Slowly, but not too slowly, the system of management would become a means of excluding experience foreign to the notation; then, in the intellectual resistance to experiential challenges to the adequacy of the models and notation, the form of management would reveal itself as a form of authoritarian control. Ervin Lazlo, like Walt Whitman Rostow before him, would simply become another academic liberal responsible for dimensions of misery beyond anything dreamt of in his philosophy.

Given the contemporary fascination with computer modeling and systems science, it shows a great deal of foresight that the World Order Models Project did not get caught up in these quick fixes. Relying more on the humanistic traditions of philosophy and international law, this transnational group of scholars has tried to initiate a discussion "On the Creation of a Just World Order." In the opinion of Professor Saul Mendlovitz, the director of the project and the president of

the Institute for World Order, such a discussion is already
overdue.

It is my considered judgement that there is no longer a
question of whether or not there will be world government
by the year 2000. As I see it, the questions we should be
addressing to ourselves are: how it will come into being—
by cataclysm, drift, more or less rational design—and
whether it will be totalitarian, benignly elitist, or participa-
tory (the probabilities being in that order).[14]

Although the World Order Models Project (which goes by
the felicitous acronymn of WOMP and thereby sets us thinking of Kurt Vonnegut) avoids the pitfalls of the Club of Rome
approach, it is still caught up in the common assumptions of
social science. It is, perhaps, unfair to ask scholars to think
wild and come up with visions of the 1990's, for that is what
we have our H. G. Wellses and Doris Lessings for, but it is a
bit surprising that these scholars seem so limited in their
imaginings of the future and their knowledge of the art, religions, and philosophies of the past. Professor Sakamoto talks
about global identity, but shows no sense of understanding
the power of myth, religion, and art in creating human identity; and this lack of cultural vision is shared by Professors
Kothari, Lagos, and Galtung.

Whether it is the Club of Rome, WOMP, the United Nations University in Tokyo, or the United Nations Institute for
Training and Research (UNITAR) in New York, it is much the
same thing: the confident assumption that the paradigms and
methodologies of social science are adequate to create a planetary culture with a built-in system of global management. In
none of these elitist associations do we find an awareness that
social science cannot hold together if it is inflated into an
entire world culture.

In the period from 1945 to 1975, America engaged in a
project of modernization of the Third World which was syn-

onymous with the Americanization of the planet. Through the work of our universities, foundations, and government, we sent our elite across the world and brought the intellectual elite of the world to study in our universities. During this thirty-year period, America was the model all others copied. But sometimes that copying was a weak cloning which created genetic monsters. When Nehru abandoned the ideas of Gandhi concerning decentralization, labor-intensive cottage industries, and sacred consciousness in satyagraha in an effort to imitate America with its capital-intensive economies of scale and secular consumer-oriented society, he laid the foundations for the mess that is modern India. If Gandhi had been followed, the difference between India and Mao's China would not be as extreme as it is today.

The disaster of India is the disaster of trying to force the American, social-science world view on the preindustrial world. With the failure of the Green Revolution in India, with the failure of the electronic battlefield in Vietnam, and with the complete failure of the whole American expedition to Vietnam, we have reached the end of that postwar era which saw the rise of modernization. If we are going to understand these failures, we must understand the limits to the kind of training social scientists receive in our universities, the limits to the epistemology and methodology upon which the social sciences are based,[15] and the limits to extending that social science throughout all our global institutions. The Club of Rome, WOMP, UNITAR, and the United Nations University in Tokyo are all collections of social scientists, managers, and civil servants. Looking back over the last six thousand years of civilization, I can't help but think that humanity deserves a better deal than out of a deck with only one suit.

Two members of the World Order Models Project clearly understand the intellectual and spiritual limitations of social science. As a professor of international law, Richard A. Falk understands the need to escape the paradigms of the professional approach, and in his seminars on world order at Princeton, he has included the prophetic novels of Doris Lessing.

Although Falk endorses the work of Lazlo, he realizes that there is more to culture than General Systems models of culture.

The human species may be better prepared for transition to a new system of world order than is generally evident, especially to those accustomed to thinking about change in the short time horizons of power wielders. Teilhard de Chardin and Sri Aurobindo, among others, have discerned a shift in human sentiment toward solidarity and altruism, and we believe that this shift is one significant feature of our generally bleak modern situation. Just as the collapse of colonialism was comprehensible only after it happened, so might the collapse or displacement of the state system become visible only when we get a chance to look backward. The call for a world order more responsive to bioethical requirements—species survival, including habitability of the planet—represents a new impulse in human history, itself a hopeful sign.[16]

The German contributor to WOMP, Professor C. F. von Weizsäcker, takes the most interesting stance of all the members of the project; significantly, he entitles his essay "A Skeptical Contribution." What separates von Weizsäcker from his more liberal colleagues is his vision of evil. Von Weizsäcker is not a social scientist, but a physicist, and so his standards of scientific rigor do not allow him to be content with the general level of discussion in the behavioral sciences; but as a physicist who had to work under close surveillance by the Nazis during the war, von Weizsäcker has had a more firsthand experience of terror and the demonic in the management of an advanced industrial state, and it is this experience which seems to give his work a tone of authority beyond that of Professors Galtung, Lagos, or Sakamoto. Von Weizsäcker's caveat needs to be taken seriously by all world reformers.

In many religions the concept of the radically evil is found. Psychoanalysis uses a structurally similar concept, that of neurotic compulsion. Ambivalence is familiar in neurotic behavior. On a conscious level, a neurotic can perfectly well set some value at an exaggerated pedestal and at the same time on an unconscious level be hostile to this value and unknown to himself hinder its realization with all the means at his disposal. Is the ambivalence of history a neurosis of mankind? But how shall we judge if this is so? . . .

Paradoxical as it may seem from purely political or social analysis, I am convinced that our actual task, on whose success the possibility of a true world peace stands or falls, is the realization of the Human Self. One of its forms is the achievement of religion in its truth, to which the meeting of cultures and religions may contribute.[17]

The Buddhists would indeed say that mankind is neurotic and subject to neurotic compulsions. The world-transforming idealist is as neurotic as the rest, and does, as von Weizsäcker suggests, work against himself. The cause of suffering, says the *Dhamapada,* is attachment. What would happen to the political activist if he could not rush about doing good and reforming the world, but had to sit every day in meditation? Would he begin to look, not just *at* his thoughts, but *behind* his thoughts? Would he begin to see, in calling his whole assumptions of reality into question, that he himself is the evil he is fleeing? Do we have time to wait while he sits before he rises again to change the world?

Precisely because the world is running out of time we no longer have time to let the world-transformer do anything else. It took sixteen centuries to go from the Sermon on the Mount to the Inquisition, but it took only a few decades to go from Marx in the British Museum to Stalin and the death camps in Siberia. Things are even more accelerated now, so we could go from the creation of a just world order to an authoritarian world order in a few years. If we are going to have a new planetary culture, and not simply a world order pieced together out of American social science, Soviet police controls, Japanese productivity, and Brazilian ambition, then we will need something more than national politics raised to a transnational level. Let the political activist take a few hours out of his day to become a student of consciousness through meditation.

We seem to be in the early, ideological stages of a global revolution, at a time when the thinkers, visionaries, and disaffected gather in coffeehouses to discuss the prospects for a change in the order of things. Let us assume that this process will continue. New works of art will appear by artists with an increasingly planetary vision. We already have the music of Stockhausen, the novels of Doris Lessing, the poetry of Gary Snyder, and the sculpture and architecture of Paolo Soleri; let us assume that new artists join this group, and that philosophers, historians, and doctors of jurisprudence follow. Slowly, as the movement begins to take on the qualities of a planetary renaissance, it will be joined by, let us say, a Member of Parliament in Canada, a Prime Minister from New Zealand, an American Congresswoman, and a governor of a state. As the political dimension to the planetary renaissance begins to develop, a cry goes up for mobilization, parties, platforms, and candidates. Suddenly we are no longer in the coffeehouse days of discussing planetary culture at Zen Center in San Francisco, Lindisfarne in New York, or New Alchemy in Massachusetts; we are at the stage when individuals want to use these places to "lend a little New Age lustre" to a particular candidate's political campaign. If the planetary thinkers enter the old politics-as-usual game of campaigns and candidates, the routinization of charisma will have begun, and the new thought will simply be a linear extension of the old liberalism of McGovern, McCarthy, or Kennedy.

But perhaps this process of routinization is inevitable, and part of the historical process of change. Perhaps it is wrong to hold back from politics in a purist's concern for one's spiritual virginity; perhaps sacrifice is necessary and new waves of thought must be smashed upon the beach so that other waves can come in to wash out every ripple one has made upon the sand. In the days when JFK was leading "the best and the brightest" from Harvard to Washington, who would have thought that Arthur Schlesinger, Jr., McGeorge Bundy, and Walt Whitman Rostow would turn out to be men of such limited vision and unlimited arrogance? After years of institutionalized mediocrity, it took one's breath away to think that Harvard and Washington could join together.

All that is history now, but have we really learned the lesson from it? Are not the new cries for world order simply an extension of the postwar doctrine of modernization? Now instead of the elimination of tribal society, it is national cultures that are the targets. Which is the truer step toward the creation of a just world order: the spiritual realization of the Human Self, of which von Weizsäcker speaks, or the rational creation of a world government by the year 2000, of which Mendlovitz speaks? Which is better: global politics emerging out of the paradigms of social science or planetary culture arising from an evolutionary transformation of consciousness? In the summer of 1974 at a conference at Lindisfarne, the debate between myself and Professor Mendlovitz went on for ten days. It was an agon: both of us were simultaneously right and wrong.

A transcendental mysticism which negates all political activity is a self-defensive ideology created by contemplatives who have stopped along the way in the process of meditation. Right Livelihood is one of the truths of the Buddhist Eightfold Path, and in the Zen ox-herding pictures, the pilgrim returns to the city from sunyata with bliss-bearing hands. So we must have right politics as part of our right livelihood.

In fact, right politics can only spring from right livelihood. If we have an industrial nation-state in which greed and the lust for power are what everyman thinks is "reality," if we have a business which regards the transformation of a forest into a parking lot as a sign of progress, then we will have a nation of businessmen run by businessmen for businessmen, and Nixon and Watergate will be the politics it deserves. In the world of karma, there are no victims, only fellow criminals. Jefferson understood that right politics could come only out of right livelihood, and so he rejected industry and urbanization as a foundation of the new republic.

> This reliance cannot deceive us, as long as we remain virtuous; and I think we shall be so, as long as agriculture is our principal object, which will be the case, while there remain vacant lands in any part of America. When we get piled upon one another in large cities, as in Europe, we shall become corrupt as in Europe, and go to eating one another as they do there.[18]

As different as Jefferson, Gandhi, and Mao are from one another, they are alike in their rejection of urbanization, industrialization, and capital-intensive economies of scale. If we are entering a period of "The Limits to Growth" and the general economic crisis of industrial society, perhaps we should explore a global convergence of the thought of Jefferson, Gandhi, and Mao.

Jefferson chose the farmer because the farmer lived in cooperation with nature and lived on a scale in which nature was great and man was in just proportion. Jefferson was looking toward an ideal agrarian republic, an ideal he never could realize. He vacillated over the issue of freeing the slaves, and he was never able to put Monticello on a sound economic footing. He was a much better ambassador in urban Paris and a much better President in urban Washington than he was a country squire in rural Virginia. But for all his contradictions (and in his contradictions he is, again, like Gandhi and Mao), I think Jefferson is the most prophetic voice for our future as we look back to our revolutionary origins in the Bicentennial.

In contemporary America, 2 percent of the population feed the remaining 98 percent, who are indeed piled upon one another in large cities. In Mao's China, 85 percent are involved in food production. The modern American businessman is proud that only 2 percent feed the rest, and he warns, along with his representatives, President Ford and Secretary of Agriculture Butz, that if the Arabs get tough with fuel, we will fight back with food. Unfortunately, neither Ford nor Butz realizes, as Howard Odum and John Todd do,[19] that we grow our potatoes with oil and dry our corn with natural gas. The impending crisis of industrialized agriculture will strike the *hubris* of the Americans, and the lines at the gas stations a year ago will be matched by long lines at the supermarkets in all our great cities. Then the famine will come home to us with a vengeance.

Marx may have complained about "the idiocy of rural life," and might have scoffed at Jefferson's yeomen, Lenin's serfs, and Mao's peasants, but we are going to have to go back to the country whether we like it or not. Urbanization simply cannot go on without turning the once great cities like New York into Calcuttas. But with modern electronics and miniaturized technology, we do not have to return to the idiocy of the nineteenth-century rural landscape, and here is where Jefferson speaks to our contemporary condition.

Monticello may have failed as a tobacco farm run by slaves, but as a center of scientific research and artistic creation it was a prophetic intuition of a new kind of community. The pattern for the Enlightenment and the Romantic Era was the solitary genius whose mind was in the sky while the peasants around him put their hands in the soil. But both Gandhi and Mao generated a new myth for a new age, or, rather, they went back to the Rule of Benedict and gave new life to an old myth. Gandhi spun and Mao toiled with the peasants, and when the commissars and professors lost touch with the earth and the elemental life, Mao sent them back to toil again with the peasants. The return to the meta-industrial village need not be a return to the idiocy and drudgery of the preindustrial village. History is a spiral, not a circle; as we spiral back to the country, we can pick up the old labor and turn it into a sacred ritual and a form of art. In a planetary village, communal labor can become a ritual that brings the community together in sacred work for only a few hours a day; the rest of the day can be given over to works of spiritual and intellectual creation, not the isolated creations of the solitary genius, but the individual creations of a community of Pythagorean scientists and contemplative artists and scholars.

In a planetary village of contemplatives, nature could be great, the machines tiny, and man in just proportion between the two. No longer need there be economies of scale in which massive amounts of fossil fuel are used to grow wheat in vast acreages so that huge trucks can burn gasoline to take flour into the enormous cities where great factories can make Ritz Crackers that can then be trucked again to the airports so that jumbo jets can fly them down to Venezuela where multinational forms of advertising can convince the peasants to abandon their locally made tortillas in favor of the creations of Nabisco. No longer would Madison Avenue heat up the economy so that shoddily built goods with built-in obsolescence could destroy nonrenewable resources and produce disastrous pollution. In industrial society, you are what you own. In contemplative cultures, your being is the source of your identity. Contemplatives need less, consume less, and therefore can produce less. No man need labor eight hours a day at the same dreary task of putting a door on a Cadillac. In industrial culture, poverty is a disgrace; in contemplative culture, poverty is the elegance of simplicity. As long as we continue to live in industrial culture, we will need an authoritarian government to control unemployment, create jobs, subsidize the auto industry, and strip-mine the Dakotas so that America can becomes one continental Los Angeles. If we have a spiritual transformation and create a meta-industrial culture, the drastic solutions of mass government will be unnecessary.

Once again, Thomas Jefferson was right when he said:

"That government is best which governs least." Right politics must grow out of right livelihood. If we try to impose an elitist political solution to world problems, we will encounter the inherent resistance of human nature. In despair at the ignorant resistance of the people, the political elite, established or revolutionary, would fall back upon force as a means of achieving its ends. The meta-industrial culture cannot be created by massive intervention of government; the transformation of world culture will spring from the depths of the unconscious of the human race and will be expressed in myth through the visions and creations of individuals. The Papacy did not create the Renaissance, and the White House will not create the planetary renaissance.

Let us assume that a movement toward right livelihood among a creative minority begins to grow at a time when the crisis of industrial civilization is becoming apparent to a much larger minority. The groups begin to gather and speak of a Planetary Constitutional Convention. It is precisely at this point that the problem of evil will have to be dealt with. The constitutional convention of the planetary "good guys" would contain the seed-form for the greatest tyranny in the history of mankind. The new liberals would proclaim their good intentions, and then go on to create a horror much worse than Vietnam.

The first act of the Planetary Constitutional Convention must be to come to terms with the evil of their meeting in the first place. The convention must contemplate its own shadow and take in the projections of evil onto the "bad guys" in the nation-states. They must realize that they themselves are the bad guys. In full consciousness of their own evil, they then should affirm that no act is good unless its goodness is seen in the immediacy of the act. An act which justifies itself by appealing to a later good is a delusion left over from the old industrial, atomistic world view in which all things were separate and unrelated. Everything prehends everything else, as Whitehead argued. The murder of Diem leads to the murder of the Kennedy brothers; the temporary dictatorship of the proletariat becomes the permanent dictatorship of the ex-proletariat. Unless the Good is seen shining in the immediacy of the act, it should not be adopted. All appeals to reason, expediency, and necessity are appeals to the very forces that wreck all ideals. One must have courage and be willing to take risks; no one can love who has not known his own terror; that is what the temptation, the crucifixion, and the resurrection of Christ are all about. The ego tries for its own protection to strike a bargain and make some reasonable compromises, but only the Soul or the Daimon can make a sacrifice out of love. Sacrifice means to make sacred; in politics, we may be called upon to make sacrifices for the Good, but we should make no compromises with it. As every martyr has recognized, it is better to die nobly for an ideal than to survive ignobly for "reality," for by that process of compromise, reality is continually deprived of ideality, until nothing is left but ignobility, and thus nothing is left to live for. Nietzsche was no Christian martyr, but even he realized that "Man would sooner have the void for a purpose than be void of purpose."

Evil will arise in the Planetary Constitutional Convention because of the contradictory nature of reality, the nature in which all institutions subvert the values for which they are founded, and in which all values are achieved in conflict with their opposites.[20] Therefore, in the vision of Jefferson, contradiction must be countered with constitution.

All powers of government, legislative, executive, and judiciary, result to the legislative body. The concentrating these in the same hands is precisely the definition of despotic government. It will be no alleviation that these will be exercised by a plurality of hands, and not by a single one. Let those who doubt it turn their eyes on the republic of Venice. As little will it avail us that they are chosen by ourselves. An elective despotism was not the government we fought for, but one which should not only be founded on free principles, but in which the powers of government should be so divided and balanced among several bodies of magistracy, as that no one could transcend their legal limits, without being effectually checked and restrained by the others.[21]

Jefferson knew that there was every chance in the world for the Revolution to betray itself; he knew the American people could go from servitude to King George to servitude to King George Washington. He had seen Patrick Henry go from being a patriot crying "Give me liberty or give me death" to an egotist conspiring to become military dictator of Virginia. So much like a Platonic sage, Jefferson would have preferred to stay at home to be the philosopher-king of Monticello, but he could see that if he did nothing, the American Revolution would fail and in the chaos of its ending confirm every crowned head in Europe of the wisdom of the rule of God's anointed.

With the popular idolization of General Washington, with the ambitions of Patrick Henry, and with the Alien and Sedition Acts of Adams's government, Jefferson had enough experience to see that the tendency of every movement is to progress toward its opposite. With tough-mindedness he knew that all single forces would move, if unchecked, into corruption, and so he sought to set up a system of ritual conflict in a constitution; but he also knew that no constitution could be perfect, and so, much like Mao after him, this American revolutionary affirmed the permanence of revolution and believed that the Constitution should be reachieved in every generation so that the world could belong to the living, and not the noble dead, be they kings or revolutionaries.[22]

Constitutionalism has its rigidities, and there is much to be said in favor of British Common Law over Jeffersonian liberalism. But since the enforced resignation of President Nixon, America has shown a flexibility that matches the dialectic of the British system with its "Loyal Opposition" and "Shadow Cabinets." There is some hope that a just world order could draw on the best of both the traditions of Common Law and Jeffersonian liberalism.

Because the American governmental system, much like the Mexican, has tended to devolve into a one-party system, there has been a marked ideological tendency in both countries to think that there is the Truth, and that all else is heresy and subversion. Consequently, the true dynamic of opposition has shifted to the world political scene, where capitalism and communism are the major contending forces. Any Planetary Constitutional Convention will have to recognize the simultaneous truth of the opposed ideologies of a free-market system and a planned economy.

If we wish to understand the rise of a new world order, it might be useful to look back to the sixteenth century, when the present world system came into being. According to Immanuel Wallerstein's account, the world economy is an organism in which conflict is part of its systemic nature.

> A world-system is a social system, one that has boundaries, structures, member groups, rules of legitimation, and coherence. Its life is made up of the conflicting forces which hold it together by tension, and tear it apart as each group seeks eternally to remold it to its advantage. It has the characteristics of an organism, in that it has a life-span over which its characteristics change in some respects and remain stable in others. One can define its structures as being at different times strong or weak in terms of the logic of its functioning. . . .
>
> It is further argued that thus far there have only existed two varieties of such world systems: world empires, in which there is a single political system over most of the area, however attenuated the degree of its effective control; and those systems in which such a single political system does not exist over all, or virtually all, of the space. For

convenience and for want of a better term, we are using the
term "world economy" to describe the latter . . .

It is the peculiarity of the modern world-system that a
world economy has survived for 500 years and yet has not
come to be transformed into a world empire—a peculiarity
that is the secret of its strength.[23]

As Wallerstein describes the two varieties of world systems,
it begins to be obvious that these two models are not casual,
chance expressions of randomly shifting historical circumstances; rather, the two models are archetypes, and their archetypal nature argues that even the formation of world systems is the expression of the collective unconscious of the
human race. Whether it is dynamic Athens against monolithic
and imperial Persia, as described in Herodotus; or Athens
against Sparta, as described in Thucydides; or the United
States against the Soviet Union, it is the case of a creatively
unstable system against a stable but creatively stagnant empire.

The archetypal nature of this battle is also seen in two very
different mythological expressions: the popular science-
fiction TV show, *Star Trek*, and the ancient Babylonian creation epic, the *Enuma Elish*. In *Star Trek* the cold war is projected onto the planetarium screen of the stars in the form of
the battle of the Federation and the Klingon Empire; the
description of each world system sounds as if it were taken
from the pages of Wallerstein. In the Babylonian epic, the
Great Mother, Tiamat, is presented as the slothful beast who
loves the quiet and rest of primeval time and resents the noisy
parties of the new dancing gods. She calls to her weak male
consort to help her destroy the young gods so that they can
return in peace to their primordial sleep. Here the feminine
principle is seen as the image of entropy, and the dancing
gods, the forms of the planets, as the active principle of matter in motion. The young gods elect a champion, Marduk, the
male principle, to protect them. Marduk sets out to challenge
the rule of the Negative Mother; he is the active male god who

can create the magic form to surround the gods to protect them from the chaos that wears away at their edges; he can recite the magic word and through the power of logos tear the fabric and put it back together again. Marduk slays the Great Mother and out of the bits and pieces of her body builds the great city of Babylon. This movement from chaos to polis, parallel to the same development in the *Oresteia,* is an evolutionary development against entropy. Life is the expression of a creative disequilibrium; all is motion and transformation, but in this disequilibrium there is a great deal of internal conflict. In the imperial system of Tiamat there is a fear of conflict and noise and an inability to tolerate ambiguity; all must be forced into sameness, into the unconscious oneness that is heat-death and entropy.

In the cold war we projected these archetypal patterns onto the screen of history. The great bear of the Soviet Union wished to repress all conflict so that it could go back to its long Russian winter sleep. It was an empire and worked to extend its uniformity everywhere; if Hungary or Czechoslovakia became creative and dynamic, it moved to smash difference into sameness with tanks. America, by contrast, was the noisy, transforming active principle; with energy and vulgarity it ran amok on the planet, selling Coca-Cola and computers, and putting McDonald's hamburger stands in Paris and the Stars and Stripes on the moon.

In fighting with one another, America and Russia experienced a passionate exchange of characteristics. We moved in the direction of a planned economy, and they came to us in search of innovation, new technology, and credits to finance their own modernization. If either America or the Soviet Union were to win over the other in peace, the world would stagnate into a monolithic, bureaucratic, socialist industrial system. If either were to go to war with the other, the world system would simply be destroyed. Thus the Nixon-Kissingerian strategy of détente seems to be the logical extension of the modern world system as described by Wallerstein.

Strong states serve the interests of some groups and hurt those of others. From however the standpoint of the world-system as a whole, if there is to be a multitude of political entities (that is, if the system is not a world-empire), then it cannot be the case that all these entities be equally strong. For if they were, they would be in the position of blocking the effective operation of transnational economic entities whose locus was in another state. It would then follow that the world division of labor would be impeded, the world-economy decline, and eventually the world-system fall apart.

It also cannot be that *no* state machinery is strong. For in such a case, the capitalist strata would have no mechanisms to protect their interests, guaranteeing their property rights, assuring various monopolies, spreading losses among the larger population, etc.[24]

One can see why ecologists like Howard Odum feel impelled to describe the world in the models of General Systems Theory, for in many ways the world system presents the features of a climax forest. It is obvious from everything that I have ever written that I am viscerally repelled by the systems-management approach to reality; yet, in spite of my distaste, I am forced to recognize that these house stewards of the planet are here to stay. I see them as the routine-operational force and hope to see them checked by the opposite charismatic-ideational force of Pythagorean science and the esoteric traditions of the great universal religions. If the Club of Rome and the United Nations University were to be the only expressions of global culture, then the culture of the world would be reduced to social science. From Howard Odum's point of view, this would be progress, for he feels the world would be greatly improved if priests and ministers were trained in systems science.

We may encourage faster religious change even now by injecting large doses of systems science into the training of religious leaders. . . . Let us inject systems science in over-doses into the seminaries and see what happens. Why should we fear that deviation from rigid symbols of the old religion is deviation from morality? A new and more pow-erful morality may emerge through the dedication of the millions of men who have faith in the new networks and endeavor zealously for them. Prophet where art thou?[25]

Odum's misunderstanding of the nature of revelation and the role of the unconscious in culture in the creation of new myths is to be expected, and it is precisely this willingness on the part of the systems scientist to extend his system to in-clude all areas of culture that is likely to be a feature of the creation of a new world order based on General Systems Theory. The systems scientist cannot help but think in terms of his flow charts; every area of experience simply becomes another input with another feedback loop. Religion simply becomes just one more input into *his* system. This attempt of the ego to force the unconscious to flow into its model is likely to generate a rather apocalyptic, ego-shattering experience for the individual or civilization which tries it. Odum is calling for a prophet, but he doesn't really want to see one, for he is really looking in the mirror and trying on a new set of robes to see if systems science can take on the prophetic role in culture.

Systems management is trying to surround culture, but culture must always surround management. The mystic knows, in Whitehead's terms, that consciousness cannot be "simply located" in a management system or a culture. Our new technology is unmanageable because we are trying to relate to it through management science, when we should really relate to it through mysticism. When a technology is surrounded by an uncanny and mystical consciousness, it becomes fully humanized and begins to fit man as a fist-hatchet fits his grip. Whether it is a stone ax, an airplane, a motorcycle, or a Saturn rocket, the man who excels in using a machine is the individual who has become one with it, not by becoming a machine, but by surrounding the instrument with the light web of his consciousness. All the ancient mystical techniques of the past—Yoga, Sufism, Tibetan and Zen Buddhism, Yaqui shamanism, and Gnosticism—have exploded into mass, global popularity because they are precisely what we need to surround our electronic technology with the light web of human consciousness. The mystic and the systems manager are, therefore, the archetypal polarities of the new age of planetary culture.

Culture evolves through the collusion of conflicting opposites. In medieval culture the opposites were the knight and the priest, the sword and the cross. In converting England from savagery to Christian civilization, King Oswald and St. Aidan served as the polarities of a newly emerging culture. In the shift from Christendom to commercial civilization in the Industrial Revolution, there was a shift of the poles, and the new opposites became the artist and the industrialist. While a Beethoven or a Blake ranged through new worlds of consciousness on the frontiers of culture, the industrialists drove railroads across continents, steamships across seas, and, with the Suez Canal, celebrated the wedding of Europe and Asia.

Now in the shift to meta-industrial society, or planetary culture, the artist and the industrialist have become the hierarchy of the established church of postindustrial society, and, thus, they have lost their charisma. Paintings decorate banks, poets give readings at the inaugurations of Presidents, and entrepreneurs have reached the limits to growth as the world economy begins to consolidate. Now the polarities are the mystic and the systems manager. On the charismatic-ideational side of planetary culture, we have Sri Aurobindo and Teilhard de Chardin; on the routine-operational side, we have Forrester, Meadows, Peccei, Mesarovic, Lazlo, and Odum.

In medieval culture, the militarism of the knight had to be checked. In industrial culture, the exploitations of the capitalist had to be checked. Now in planetary culture, it is the all-inclusiveness of the systems manager that must be checked. The systems theorist who is more aware of the epistemological limits of systems science, of precisely those overly confident extensions into design and conscious purpose in evolution, is Gregory Bateson. Oddly enough, Odum, Lazlo, and Jantsch seem to be ignorant of Bateson's classic paper.[26]

> We get a picture, then, of mind as synonymous with cybernetic system—the relevant total information-processing trial-and-error completing unit. And we know that within Mind in the widest sense there will be a hierarchy of sub-systems, any one of which we can call an individual mind.
>
> But this picture is precisely the same as the picture which I arrived at in discussing *the unit of evolution* [namely, the organism plus the environment]. I believe that this identity is the most important generalization which I have to offer you tonight. . . .
>
> It means, you see, that I now localize something which I am calling "Mind" immanent in the large biological system, the ecosystem. . . .
>
> The cybernetic epistemology which I have offered you would suggest a new approach. The individual mind is immanent but not only in the body. It is immanent also in pathways and messages outside the body; and there is a larger Mind of which the individual mind is only a subsystem. This larger Mind is comparable to God and is perhaps what some people mean by "God," but it is still immanent in the total interconnected social system and planetary ecology.[27]

The tongue cannot taste itself,[28] the mind cannot know itself, and the system cannot model itself. As Bateson has argued, a TV screen cannot pass on information as to how it is processing the information without creating a larger screen, and thus involving us in a regress ad infinitum. All the information cannot get onto the screen of consciousness, and so the brain must shut out the whole if it is to process the bits. Therefore no systems science can ever model a culture, much less manage it. What the little mind of the ego cannot know, the Mind of the Self can experience in samadhi. The creation of a just world order will, thus, not come about through social science or systems science; it is already coming about through the spiritual transformation of consciousness in the Mind of humanity in resonance with the Mind of God.

The debate between Bateson and Odum is really the debate over whether a Confucian or a Taoist model should become the basis for the new culture. In the Confucian system, we would have everything based upon the ecological balance, the propriety of *Li*; this quality of *Li* would then be maintained by a global elite, a new mandarinism of civil servants and managers trained in systems science. In the Taoist model, there would be a separation of authority from power. The sage would not rule, and culture would not be identical with the activities of the imperial court. The Tao would flow as the ultimate moral order beyond human ideologies, but in the lower world it would express its flow through the opposites of yin and yang.

From the Taoist point of view the cries for world order as expressed by Odum and Lazlo represent a misunderstanding of the true world order, the Tao. If we understand that no ideology can contain the truth, then our enemy is no longer feared and hated, but cherished as our opponent who brings us closer to the realization of our being in drawing us forth to conflict. If we withdraw our projections on our enemies and take them back into ourselves, we learn compassion in the contemplation of our own shadow; and in that compassion we begin to get a glimmering of what Jesus meant when he counseled us to love our enemies. Out of that initiation into compassion through pain and terror comes an understanding of the true mystery of human love; and if we try to create a just world order with anything less than this mystery, all our clever problem-solving will be in vain, and our very efforts to do good will create a planetary evil beyond anything we have experienced before in human history.

Notes

I. Meditation on the Dark Ages, Past and Present

1. Herman Kahn and Anthony Weiner, *The Year 2000: A Framework for Speculation on the Next Thirty-Three Years* (New York: Macmillan, 1967). Zbigniew Brzezinski, *Between Two Ages: America's Role in the Technetronic Era* (New York: Viking, 1970).
2. Arthur C. Clarke, *The City and the Stars* (New York: Macmillan, 1953).
3. Kathleen Freeman, *Ancilla to the Pre-Socratics* (Cambridge: Harvard, 1962), p. 19.
4. Homer, *The Iliad*, trans. Richmond Lattimore, Book XII, 11. 1–33 (Chicago: University of Chicago, 1961).
5. R. M. Adams, *The Evolution of Urban Society* (Chicago: Aldine, 1966).
6. Letter to the Ephesians, 6:12.
7. W. K. C. Guthrie, *A History of Greek Philosophy:* Volume One, *The Earlier Presocratics and the Pythagoreans* (New York: Cambridge University Press, 1971), p. 254.
8. Marshall McLuhan, *Understanding Media* (New York: McGraw-Hill, 1966).
9. Charles F. Hockett and Robert Ascher, "The Human Revolution," in Yehudi Cohen's *Man in Adaptation:* Volume One, *The Biosocial Background* (Chicago: Aldine, 1968), p. 216.
10. Lucy Menzies, *St. Columba of Iona* (Glasgow: The Iona Community, 1974), p. 45.
11. Hans Wingler, *The Bauhaus: Weimar, Dessau, Berlin, Chicago* (Cambridge: M.I.T. Press, 1969).
12. Pierre Teilhard de Chardin, *The Future of Man* (New York: Harper & Row, 1969), p. 130.

13. See my *Passages About Earth: An Exploration of the New Planetary Culture*, Chapter Seven (New York: Harper & Row, 1974).

14. John Pfeiffer, *The Emergence of Man* (New York: Harper & Row, 1969), p. 332.

15. See E. F. Schumacher, *Small Is Beautiful: Economics as if People Mattered* (New York: Harper & Row, 1974).

16. As quoted in *Thomas Jefferson on Democracy*, ed. Saul K. Padover (New York: Appleton-Century-Crofts, 1939), p. 69.

17. Saul Bellow, "Machines and Storybooks: Literature in the Age of Technology," *Harper's Magazine*, August, 1974, pp. 48–59.

18. Gunther S. Stent, *The Coming of the Golden Age: A View of the End of Progress* (New York: The American Museum of Natural History, 1969).

19. *Newsweek*, November 4, 1974, p. 69. The ideas of miniaturization used in this essay come from Teilhard de Chardin (see *Man's Place in Nature* [New York: Harper & Row, 1966], p. 47), and from Paolo Soleri's development of Chardin in *Arcology: The City in the Image of Man* (Cambridge: M.I.T. Press, 1969).

III. Three Wise Men of Gotham

1. Emmanuel C. Mesthene, *Technological Change: Its Impact on Man and Society* (Cambridge: Harvard Press, 1970), p. 60.

2. B. F. Skinner, *Beyond Freedom and Dignity* (New York: Knopf, 1971), p. 214.

3. José Delgado, M.D., *The Physical Control of the Mind: Toward a Psychocivilized Society* (New York: Harper & Row, 1969), p. 145.

4. *Ibid.*, p. 142.

5. *Ibid.*, p. 121.

6. *Ibid.*, p. 215.

7. *Ibid.*, p. 42.

8. *Ibid.*, p. 40.

9. T. S. Eliot, *The Waste Land*, 11. 360–366, in *Collected Poems, 1909–1962* (New York: Harcourt Brace Jovanovich, 1963).

10. Robert Keith Wallace and Herbert Benson, "The Physiology of Meditation," *Scientific American*, February, 1972, pp. 84–92.

IV. Occulture: Out of Sight, Out of Mind

1. Claude Lévi-Strauss, *Tristes Tropiques* (New York: Atheneum, 1964), p. 396.'

2. John C. Lilly, *The Mind of the Dolphin: A Non-Human Intelligence* (New York: Avon, 1969), p. 35.

V. Introductions to Findhorn

1. The Findhorn Foundation, *The Findhorn Garden* (New York: Harper & Row, 1975).
2. *Changing Images of Man,* Policy Report 4, The Center for the Study of Social Policy, Stanford Research Institute (Menlo Park, Calif., May, 1974), p. 143.
3. *Ibid.*, p. 17.
4. See John Todd, "The Dilemma Beyond Tomorrow," *The Journal of the New Alchemists,* Vol. II, 1974, pp. 122–128.
5. Richard J. Barnett and Ronald E. Müller, *Global Reach: The Power of the Multinational Corporations* (New York: Simon & Schuster, 1974), p. 338.
6. Pierre Teilhard de Chardin, *The Phenomenon of Man* (New York: Harper & Row, 1961), p. 30.
7. Jonas Salk, *The Survival of the Wisest* (New York: Harper & Row, 1973), p. 62.
8. *Ibid.*, p. 82.
9. David Spangler, *Revelation: The Birth of a New Age* (Findhorn, 1971), p. 59.
10. Daniel Callahan, *The Tyranny of Survival: On a Society of Technological Limits* (New York: Macmillan, 1973).

VII. The Ends of Art

1. See Saul Bellow, "Machines and Storybooks," *op. cit.*
2. Lewis Thomas, *The Lives of a Cell: Notes of a Biology Watcher* (New York: Viking, 1974), p. 142.

VIII. Evil and World Order

1. See John Todd, "The Dilemma Beyond Tomorrow," *New Alchemy Journal,* See also Mihajlo Mesarovic and Eduard Pestel, *Mankind at the Turning Point: The Second Report to the Club of Rome* (New York: Dutton, 1974), p. 115.
2. *On the Creation of a Just World Order,* ed. Saul Mendlovitz (New York: Free Press, 1975).

3. Ervin Lazlo, *A Strategy for the Future: The Systems Approach to World Order* (New York: Braziller, 1974).

4. *Ibid.*, p. 199.

5. See my "Values and Conflict Through History" in *At the Edge of History* (New York: Harper & Row, 1971).

6. See Erich Jantsch, *Design for Evolution: Self-Organization and Planning in the Life of Human Systems* (New York: Braziller, 1975), p. 94.

7. Goethe, *Faust: Part One,* trans. Philip Wayne (London: Penguin, 1958), p. 75.

8. See my *The Imagination of an Insurrection: Dublin, Easter 1916* (New York: Oxford, 1967; Harper & Row, 1971), p. 109.

9. Peter Viereck, *Meta-Politics: The Roots of the Nazi Mind* (New York: Capricorn, 1961) p. 155.

10. C. G. Jung, *Aion: Researches into the Phenomenology of the Self,* Volume 9, II of *The Collected Works* (Princeton, 1968), p. 70.

11. *The Tibetan Book of the Dead,* trans. Francesca Freemantle and Chögyam Trungpa (Berkeley: Shambala, 1975).

12. Ervin Lazlo, *op. cit.,* p. 225.

13. Ludwig von Bertalanffy, *General System Theory* (London: Penguin, 1971), p. 10.

14. Saul Mendlovitz, *op. cit.,* p. xvi.

15. See Chapters Five and Six of my *Passages About Earth, op. cit.*

16. Richard A. Falk, in Mendlovitz, *op. cit.,* p. 220.

17. C. F. von Weizsäcker in Mendlovitz, *ibid.,* pp. 131, 150.

18. *Thomas Jefferson on Democracy,* ed. Saul K. Padover (New York: Appleton-Century-Crofts, 1939), p. 70.

19. See John Todd, *op. cit.;* also Howard T. Odum, *Environment, Power, and Society* (New York: Wiley, 1971), pp. 116, 119–120.

20. See footnote 5.

21. Thomas Jefferson, *Notes on the State of Virginia* (New York: Harper & Row, 1964), p. 113.

22. See Fawn Brodie, *Thomas Jefferson: An Intimate History* (New York: Norton, 1974), *passim.*

23. Immanuel Wallerstein, *The Modern World-System: Capitalist Agriculture and the Origins of the European World-Economy in the Sixteenth Century* (New York: Academic Press, 1974), pp. 347, 348.

24. *Ibid.,* p. 354.

25. Howard T. Odum, *op. cit.*, p. 310.
26. See Gregory Bateson, "The Effects of Conscious Purpose on Human Adaptations" in *Steps to an Ecology of Mind* (New York: Ballantine, 1972), p. 440.
27. *Ibid.*, pp. 460, 461.
28. Chögyam Trungpa, *Cutting Through Spiritual Materialism* (Berkeley: Shambala, 1974), p. 183.

About the Author

William Irwin Thompson received his B.A. from Pomona College and his Ph.D. from Cornell University. He has held teaching positions at Cornell, MIT, and York University in Toronto. In 1973 he founded the Lindisfarne Association in Southampton, New York. In addition to *At the Edge of History,* he is also the author of *Passages About Earth, The Imagination of an Insurrection: Dublin, Easter 1916,* and he has written articles for *Harper's Magazine, The New York Times, Change,* and other publications.

About the Editor of This Series

Ruth Nanda Anshen, philosopher and editor, plans and edits *World Perspectives, Religious Perspectives, Credo Perspectives, Perspectives in Humanism,* and *The Science of Culture Series.* She also writes and lectures on the relationship of knowledge to the nature and meaning of man and his existence. Her book, *The Reality of the Devil: Evil in Man,* a study in the phenomenology of evil, is published by Harper & Row.